PODGOR
TRAVEL GUIDE 2024

Ultimate Guide to This Beautiful Gem with Amazing Natural Wonders, National parks and Beautiful Landscapes. It Includes 7-Day Itinerary For First time Visitors.

Richard Caraway

Disclaimer:

This travel guide, "Podgorica Travel Guide 2024," authored by Richard Caraway, is a product of extensive research, personal experiences, and recommendations. While every effort has been made to ensure the accuracy of the information provided, the author and the publisher make no representations or warranties of any kind, express or implied, about the completeness, accuracy, reliability, suitability, or availability of the information, products, services, or related graphics contained in this guide for any purpose.

Readers are advised to use their discretion and judgment when making travel decisions based on the information presented in this guide. The author and the publisher shall not be liable for any loss, injury, or damage arising from the use of this guide or the information contained within.

The inclusion of third-party websites, services, or products in this guide does not imply endorsement or recommendation. The author and the publisher have no control over the content, availability, or practices of third-party websites and, therefore, cannot be held responsible for any issues that may arise from accessing such external links.

Readers are encouraged to verify information independently and to seek professional advice regarding specific travel plans, safety, health, and other aspects related to their journey.

Your safety and satisfaction are of utmost importance. Enjoy your travels in Aruba responsibly, and may this guide enhance your exploration of the beautiful island.

CONTENTS

INTRODUCTION

As the December holidays approached, I gathered my wife, Laura, and our two children, Emily and Lucy, in the living room. I had promised them a memorable vacation, and it was time to reveal our destination. Excitement filled the room as they eagerly awaited the big reveal.

"Daddy, you promised us a vacation this holiday," Lucy, our youngest daughter, had reminded me earlier which made me come up with a plan and immediately call the rest of my family for a little surprise. "We want to spend Christmas in another country!"

I smiled and nodded, reaching for a small stack of papers. On each paper, I had scribbled the names of eight different places. I handed them to Lucy and asked her to pick one, her decision determining our family adventure. The suspense was palpable as we held our breath.

With a mischievous grin, Lucy reached into the pile and pulled out a slip of paper. She unfolded it carefully and read aloud, "Podgorica, Montenegro!"

A collective gasp filled the room. "We're going to Europe?" Laura exclaimed, her eyes wide with excitement.

I nodded, thrilled by the destination our youngest had chosen. "Yes, we're going to Podgorica, Montenegro. Let's embark on an unforgettable adventure!"

As our departure day approached, we eagerly packed our bags, brimming with anticipation. Leaving behind the sunny beaches of San Diego, California, we embarked on a journey to a land brimming with history, culture, and natural wonders.

When we finally arrived in Montenegro and set foot in Podgorica, we were immediately captivated. The city greeted us with open arms, its streets buzzing with life and energy. We couldn't help but exclaim, "Oh my gosh! This is a beautiful city, so clean and entertaining!"

Over the next seven days, we immersed ourselves in the wonders of Podgorica, exploring its every nook and cranny. We visited enchanting places, each holding its own unique charm.

Our first stop was the heart of the city, the vibrant Independence Square. We strolled through the square, marveling at the grand architecture and the imposing Clock Tower. The atmosphere was electric, with locals and tourists alike filling the square with laughter and conversation.

From there, we ventured to the iconic Millennium Bridge. As we stood on its sleek structure, we were treated to breathtaking views of the Moraca River. The shimmering water reflected the city's lights, creating a magical ambiance that left us in awe.

Eager to experience nature's embrace, we ventured to the Park of the Revolution. The serene green space provided respite from the bustling city, offering us a moment of tranquility. We found ourselves wandering along its winding paths, basking in the beauty of the surrounding trees and flowers.

But our adventures didn't end there. We discovered the enchantment of Skadar Lake, a true natural wonder. Boarding a boat, we cruised along its shimmering waters, marveling at the untouched beauty that surrounded us. The lake's tranquil atmosphere was punctuated by the songs of countless bird species, leaving us in a state of peaceful awe.

As our journey continued, we explored the ancient city of Stari Bar, wandering through its narrow streets and witnessing the remnants of centuries past. The ruins whispered tales of a rich history, and we found ourselves transported to another time.

No visit to Montenegro would be complete without exploring the breathtaking national parks that dotted the landscape. We ventured to Durmitor National Park, where snow-capped peaks and pristine lakes awaited us. We hiked through lush forests and stood in awe of the dramatic canyons that unfolded before our eyes.

One of the highlights of our trip was a visit to the Ostrog Monastery. Perched high on a cliff, it seemed to defy gravity. We marveled at the devotion that inspired its creation, and the spiritual energy within its walls touched our souls.

Our journey through Podgorica was a tapestry of unforgettable experiences. We savored the flavors of traditional Montenegrin cuisine, relishing in the rich aromas and vibrant spices. We danced to the rhythms of lively folk music, immersing ourselves in the country's cultural heritage.

As our time in Podgorica drew to a close, we couldn't help but feel a sense of gratitude for the memories we had created. Montenegro had exceeded our expectations, revealing itself as a hidden gem nestled in the heart of Europe.

With hearts full of wanderlust, we bid farewell to Podgorica, a city that had become a cherished part of our family's journey. As we boarded the plane back to California, we carried with us the essence of Montenegro—a place of beauty, adventure, and the indelible magic of exploration.

And thus, our travel tale unfolded, an adventure etched in our hearts forever—a testament to the power of discovery and the bonds forged through shared experiences.

CHAPTER 1

WELCOME TO PODGORICA

Overview of Podgorica as the capital city of Montenegro

Welcome to Podgorica, the captivating capital city of Montenegro. Situated at the confluence of the Ribnica and Moraca rivers, this vibrant metropolis invites you to explore its rich history, immerse yourself in its cultural heritage, and discover its natural wonders.

Podgorica serves as the administrative and economic hub of Montenegro, showcasing a fascinating blend of architectural styles that reflect its diverse past. As you wander through the city center, you'll encounter a tapestry of ancient ruins, socialist-era buildings, and modern designs. It's a testament to the city's resilience and its continuous evolution.

Beyond its architectural treasures, Podgorica has a vibrant cultural scene. Museums, galleries, and theaters provide insights into Montenegro's art, history, and performing arts. Whether you're interested in traditional folk performances or contemporary exhibitions, the city's cultural offerings will captivate you.

Nature lovers will be captivated by Podgorica's surrounding landscapes. From the tranquil shores of Lake Skadar to the rugged beauty of the Moraca River Canyon, the region provides numerous opportunities for outdoor exploration. National parks such as Biogradska Gora and Lovcen entice visitors with their pristine forests, hiking trails, and breathtaking scenery.

No visit to Podgorica is complete without sampling the flavors of Montenegrin cuisine. From hearty meat dishes to fresh seafood specialties, the local cuisine entices the palate. While enjoying the warmth of Montenegrin hospitality in local restaurants and cafes, try regional delights such as Njegusi prosciutto, Kacamak, and Pomegranate rakija.

Throughout this travel guide, we will look at different aspects of Podgorica, providing you with detailed information, insider tips, and local insights to help you enjoy your visit. Our goal is to help you create unforgettable memories in this captivating capital city by providing transportation options, accommodation recommendations, dining experiences, shopping destinations, entertainment venues, and practical advice.

Brief History and Cultural Significance:

Podgorica has a rich and complex history that stretches back thousands of years. The area has been inhabited since ancient times, with evidence of human settlements dating as far back as the Paleolithic era. Over the centuries, the region has witnessed the rise and fall of various civilizations, each leaving its mark on the city's cultural fabric.

During the Roman period, the city was known as Doclea and was a major trade and military center. The Romans built fortifications, roads, and bridges, which helped the city prosper. Traces of this era can still be seen today, with archaeological sites like the Doclea Roman Ruins providing insight into the city's ancient history.

During the Middle Ages, Podgorica and its surrounding territories were ruled by several powers, including the Byzantines, Slavic tribes, and the Serbian Nemanjić dynasty. The city's strategic location made it a sought-after prize, resulting in frequent conflicts and ownership changes.

During the Ottoman Empire's rule in the Balkans, Podgorica, then known as Birziminium, underwent significant changes. The Ottomans built a fortress and developed the city into an administrative and commercial hub. Islamic influence during this time period left an architectural imprint on the city, as evidenced by structures such as the Clock Tower and the Sahat Kula (Watchtower).

As part of the Kingdom of Montenegro, Podgorica experienced turbulent times in the nineteenth and early twentieth centuries. Bombings caused extensive damage to the city during World War II, prompting postwar reconstruction and modernization.

In 1946, Podgorica was renamed Titograd in honor of Josip Broz Tito, the leader of the Socialist Federal Republic of Yugoslavia. Within the socialist federation, the city rose to prominence as an industrial and cultural hub.

Following Montenegro's independence in 2006, the city was renamed Podgorica to reflect its historical identity. Since then, it has seen rapid development and transformation, including new infrastructure, modern buildings, and improved amenities.

Today, Podgorica symbolizes Montenegro's resilience and progress. Its cultural significance stems from its ability to connect the past and present, with historical landmarks coexisting alongside modern structures. The city's cultural scene is thriving, with theaters, museums, art galleries, and music venues providing a vibrant platform for local and international artists to showcase their work.

Montenegrins, Serbs, Albanians, Bosniaks, and other ethnic groups make up Podgorica's population, reflecting the city's cultural diversity. This diversity contributes to the city's vibrant atmosphere, in which various traditions, languages, and customs coexist peacefully.

As you explore Podgorica, you will be able to immerse yourself in its rich history and cultural heritage. From ancient ruins to museums, traditional festivals to contemporary art exhibitions, the city provides a captivating tapestry of experiences that will help you understand and appreciate Montenegro's past and present.

Geographical Location and Climate

Podgorica, the capital city of Montenegro, is situated in the southwestern part of the Balkan Peninsula. It is located at the confluence of the Ribnica and

Moraca rivers, nestled in a fertile plain surrounded by mountains and hills.

The city's strategic location makes it an ideal starting point for exploring Montenegro's natural wonders. It is about 44 kilometers (27 miles) from the Adriatic Sea, giving visitors easy access to the breathtaking coastline and picturesque coastal towns.

Podgorica has a Mediterranean climate, with influences from both the Mediterranean Sea and the inland mountainous regions. Summers are hot and dry, and winters are mild with some rain. Here's an overview of the various seasons:

Spring (March-May): Podgorica experiences pleasant temperatures, with average highs ranging from 16°C

(61°F) in March to 23°C (73°F) in May. The city is adorned with blooming flowers and lush greenery, making it an excellent time for outdoor activities and exploration of the surrounding landscapes.

Summer (June to August) in Podgorica is hot and dry, with average temperatures ranging from 25°C (77°F) to 35°C (95°F). The warmest months are July and August. It's a popular tourist season, and the city comes alive with festivals, outdoor concerts, and bustling street life. The nearby rivers and lakes provide refreshing places to cool off.

Autumn (September to November): Podgorica experiences milder temperatures, with average highs ranging from 20°C (68°F) in September to 13°C (55°F) in November. The foliage begins to change colors, providing a beautiful backdrop for outdoor activities and sightseeing.

Winter (December to February): Podgorica has relatively mild winters when compared to other European cities. The average temperature during this season ranges from 7°C (45°F) to 12°C (54°F). While snowfall is possible, it is neither frequent nor heavy. Winter is an excellent time to visit the city's cultural attractions, relax in cozy cafes, and take day trips to nearby mountain resorts for winter sports.

Podgorica receives moderate rainfall throughout the year, with the wettest months being October and November. Because of its proximity to the mountains, the city has slightly cooler temperatures than the rest of Montenegro's coast.

It is important to note that weather patterns can change, so check the forecast before your visit. Regardless of the season, Podgorica provides a diverse range of experiences and attractions that can be enjoyed all year.

Best time to visit and weather information

Choosing the best time to visit Podgorica depends on your preferences and the type of experience you seek. Here's an overview of the different seasons and weather information to help you plan your trip:

1. Spring (March to May): Spring is a wonderful time to visit Podgorica because the city is alive with blooming flowers and vibrant greenery. The weather is generally pleasant, with temperatures gradually rising. Average high temperatures range from 16°C (61°F) in March to 23°C (73°F) in May. It's the perfect time for outdoor activities, exploring the city's cultural attractions, and admiring the natural beauty of the surrounding landscapes.

2. *Summer (June–August):* Summers in Podgorica are hot and dry, with average temperatures ranging from 25°C (77°F) to 35°C (95°F). The warmest months are July and August. If you enjoy hot weather and a lively atmosphere, this is the peak tourist season, when the city is alive with festivals, outdoor events, and vibrant street life. It's an excellent time to go swimming and do other water activities in the nearby rivers and lakes.

3. *Autumn (September to November):* Fall brings milder temperatures, making it an appealing time to visit Podgorica. Average high temperatures range from 20°C (68°F) in September to 13°C (55°F) in November. The foliage begins to change color, providing a picturesque backdrop for outdoor activities and sightseeing. It's less crowded, allowing you to enjoy the city's attractions at a slower pace.

4. *Winter (December–February):* Podgorica's winters are relatively mild in comparison to other European destinations. The average temperature during this season ranges from 7°C (45°F) to 12°C (54°F). While snowfall is possible, it is neither frequent nor heavy. Winter is an excellent time to immerse yourself in the city's cultural offerings, visit museums and galleries, and relax at cozy cafes. It's also possible to take day trips to nearby mountain resorts for winter sports like skiing and snowboarding.

It is important to note that weather patterns can change, so check the forecast before your visit. Additionally, Podgorica receives moderate rainfall throughout the year, with the wettest months being October and November.

Given the climate and weather information, the best seasons to visit Podgorica are spring (March to May) and autumn (September to November). These seasons provide pleasant temperatures, fewer crowds, and the opportunity to enjoy the region's natural beauty.

Practical Information for Travelers

When planning a trip to Podgorica, it's essential to be aware of the practical information that will help you navigate the city and ensure a smooth travel experience. Here are some key details to keep in mind:

1. Currency: Montenegro's official currency is the euro (EUR). It is widely accepted in Podgorica, and major currencies can be exchanged at banks, exchange offices, and hotels. Credit cards are also commonly accepted in hotels, restaurants, and larger establishments. Smaller establishments and local markets benefit from having some cash on hand.

2. Language: Montenegro's official language is Montenegrin. However, Serbian, Bosnian, Albanian, and Croatian are all widely spoken. English is widely understood and spoken in tourist destinations, hotels, and restaurants. A basic understanding of common phrases in the local language can be useful when interacting with locals.

3. Time Zone: Podgorica uses Central European Time (CET), which is UTC+1. Montenegro uses Central European Summer Time (CEST), which is UTC+2. It is recommended that you adjust your watches and devices when you arrive.

4. Visa Requirements: Montenegro grants visa-free travel to citizens of many countries, including European Union member states, the United States, Canada, Australia, and others. However, before traveling to Montenegro, make sure to check the visa requirements for your nationality. Make sure your passport is valid for at least six months beyond your planned stay.

5. Safety: Although Podgorica is generally a safe city, it is always advisable to take common safety precautions. Keep your belongings safe, be wary of pickpockets in crowded places, and avoid displaying valuable items openly. It is best to use licensed taxis or reliable transportation services.

6. *Health and Emergency Services:* Podgorica has good healthcare facilities. In the event of a medical emergency, call 112 for an ambulance or go to the nearest hospital. It is recommended that you have travel insurance that covers medical expenses during your stay.

7. *Electrical Outlets:* In Podgorica, the standard voltage is 230V and the frequency is 50Hz. The plugs and sockets used are of type C and F, with two round pins. Consider packing a universal adapter for your electronic devices.

8. *Transportation:* Podgorica has a well-developed transportation network. Taxis, buses, and rental cars are available to help you explore the city and its surroundings. Taxis are widely available, and it is best to use licensed ones with meters. Public buses are an inexpensive way to get around the city and surrounding towns. Car rental services are also available at the airport and in the city center.

CHAPTER 2

GETTING TO PODGORICA

Transportation Options: Flights, Trains, Buses, and Car Rentals

Podgorica, as the capital city of Montenegro, is well-connected to various transportation options that make it accessible for travelers. Here are the main methods of reaching Podgorica:

1. Flights: Podgorica Airport (IATA: TGD) is the main international airport serving the city. It operates flights to and from several European destinations. Regular flights to Podgorica are operated by major airlines including Montenegro Airlines, Air Serbia, and Ryanair. The airport is about 11 kilometers (7 miles) south of the city center, and you can get there by taxi or pre-arranged transportation services available at the airport.

2. *Trains:* Podgorica's railway station is conveniently located in the city center, providing another mode of transportation. The rail network links Podgorica to a variety of domestic and international destinations. International trains connect Podgorica with cities such as Belgrade, Serbia, and Bar, Montenegro's coastal town. The train journey from Belgrade to Podgorica provides scenic views of the Montenegrin countryside. It is advisable to check train schedules and availability in advance.

3. *Buses:* Bus travel is a popular and convenient way to reach Podgorica. The city has a central bus station close to the city center that serves both domestic and international routes. Several bus companies provide regular service to and from Podgorica, connecting it to cities in Montenegro and neighboring countries such as Serbia, Croatia, and Albania. The bus network is extensive, making it a cost-effective and efficient way to get to Podgorica and explore the rest of Montenegro.

4. Car Rentals: Renting a car is a flexible option for reaching Podgorica, especially if you prefer your own transportation during your stay. Several international and local car rental companies have offices in Podgorica Airport and the city center. Renting a car allows you to explore Podgorica and the surrounding areas at your own pace. However, you must be familiar with local traffic regulations and hold a valid driver's license.

When planning your trip to Podgorica, consider cost, convenience, and personal preferences to determine the best mode of transportation for you.

International and Domestic Connections to Podgorica:

Podgorica, the capital city of Montenegro, has both international and domestic transportation connections that make it accessible for travelers. Here's an overview of the connections to Podgorica:

1. *International flights:* Podgorica Airport (IATA: TGD) is Montenegro's main international gateway. It operates flights to and from a variety of European destinations, making Podgorica easily accessible. Montenegro Airlines, Air Serbia, Ryanair, Turkish Airlines, and Austrian Airlines are some of the major airlines that fly internationally to Podgorica. Common international routes connect Podgorica to cities like Belgrade, Vienna, Istanbul, and Zurich, among others. The frequency of flights varies depending on the season, so check the flight schedules when planning your trip.

2. *Domestic Flights:* Podgorica Airport offers domestic flights connecting Podgorica to other cities in Montenegro. Montenegro Airlines offers domestic flights from Podgorica to Tivat, a coastal town known for its beautiful beaches and resorts. These domestic flights are a convenient option for travelers looking to explore Montenegro's inland capital as well as its coastal areas.

3. Train Connections: Podgorica has multiple domestic and international train routes. The train network connects Podgorica to Montenegro's main seaport, Bar, as well as Niksic, Kolasin, and Bijelo Polje. Additionally, international trains run between Podgorica and Belgrade, Serbia. The train journey from Belgrade to Podgorica provides picturesque views of the Montenegrin countryside and is popular with tourists looking for a scenic route.

4. Bus Connections: Podgorica has a robust bus network that connects to both domestic and international destinations. Several bus companies provide regular services to and from Podgorica, connecting it to cities in Montenegro and neighboring countries. Domestic travel options include bus connections to cities such as Budva, Kotor, Herceg Novi, and Ulcinj, among others. Buses connect Podgorica to cities in Serbia, Croatia, Bosnia and Herzegovina, and Albania, providing convenient regional travel options.

These international and domestic connections make Podgorica easily accessible by air, train, and bus, allowing travelers to select the best mode of transportation for their needs and itinerary.

CHAPTER 3:

EXPLORING THE CITY CENTER

Overview of the City's Layout and Main Districts

Podgorica, the capital city of Montenegro, has a rich history and a vibrant city center that offers a mix of architectural styles, cultural attractions, and lively entertainment. Here's an overview of the city's layout and its main districts:

1. Stara Varoš (Old Town) is the historical center of Podgorica. It has narrow streets, traditional homes, and historical landmarks. This district provides a glimpse into the city's history, with notable attractions including the Clock Tower, the Sahat Kula Fortress, and the remnants of the Ribnica Fortress. Stara Varoš offers a variety of cafes, restaurants, and shops to experience local culture.

2. Njegoševa Street is the main pedestrian street in the city center. It is lined with shops, boutiques, cafes, and restaurants, making it a popular hangout for both locals and tourists. This vibrant street is ideal for leisurely walks, shopping, and taking in the lively atmosphere.

3. Trg Republike (Republic Square) is the central square of Podgorica and a popular gathering place. It is surrounded by significant structures like the Montenegrin Parliament, the National Theater, and the City Hall. The square hosts a variety of cultural events, concerts, and festivals throughout the year. It's an excellent place to unwind, people-watch, and soak up the city's atmosphere.

4. Millennium Bridge and Moraca River, a Podgorica's iconic landmark spans the Moraca River. This modern bridge is known for its unique design and provides a beautiful view of the city. The riverbanks of the Moraca River are ideal for leisurely strolls, with parks and green spaces providing a tranquil environment away from the city's hustle and bustle.

5. Gorica Hill is a popular recreational area near the city center. It features beautiful walking trails, lush greenery, and panoramic views of Podgorica. The hill is home to the Millennium Forest, a large park where you can relax, picnic, or participate in outdoor activities.

6. Sports enthusiasts should visit City Stadium and Sports Center Moraca. The City Stadium is Podgorica's main football stadium, hosting a variety of sporting events and concerts. The Sports Center Moraca is a versatile indoor arena that hosts basketball games, concerts, and other cultural events.

Local or Insider Advice:

Try local cuisine: Podgorica has a variety of traditional Montenegrin dishes that are worth trying. Try local specialties such as cicvara (cornmeal), kačamak (hearty porridge), and grilled meats. Visit local restaurants and ask for recommendations to savor the flavors of Montenegrin cuisine.

Visit the local markets: Podgorica has vibrant outdoor markets where you can learn about the local culture while also finding fresh produce, local products, and handicrafts. Visit the Vjekoslav Vukčević Green Market and Voli Market to sample local ingredients and experience the bustling atmosphere.

Explore the city by bike: Podgorica is becoming more bike-friendly, and renting a bicycle is an excellent way to explore the city center and surrounding areas. Use the bike-sharing stations and designated bike lanes to discover hidden gems and enjoy a leisurely ride along the river.

Enjoy the café culture: Podgorica has a vibrant café culture, with numerous cafés and outdoor terraces spread throughout the city. Take a break, sip a cup of coffee, and enjoy people-watching while immersing yourself in local culture.

Attend cultural events: Podgorica hosts a variety of cultural events, such as music festivals, art exhibitions, and theatrical performances. Keep an eye out for upcoming events and immerse yourself in the city's vibrant culture.

Podgorica's city center combines history, modernity, and local charm. Exploring its distinct districts, embracing local culture, and seeking insider advice will improve your experience and allow you to truly appreciate the city's beauty.

Must-Visit Landmarks and Attractions in Podgorica City Center

1. Podgorica City Hall:

Podgorica City Hall, located in the city center, is an impressive architectural gem and a significant symbol of the city. This elegant building from the early twentieth century combines neoclassical and Renaissance architectural styles. Its grand facade, adorned with decorative elements and sculptures, makes it a well-known landmark in Podgorica. While the City Hall is primarily used as the administrative center for the local government, visitors can enjoy the exterior beauty and take memorable photographs.

2. Millennium Bridge:

The Millennium Bridge is an iconic symbol of Podgorica, connecting the old and new parts of the city. This cable-stayed bridge spans the Moraca River and is known for its unique design, which features a slender pylon supporting the main span. The bridge is illuminated at night, resulting in a breathtaking visual spectacle. Walking across the Millennium Bridge provides a panoramic view of the city, including Gorica Hill and the surrounding landscapes. It is a popular spot for both locals and visitors to take a leisurely stroll and photograph breathtaking scenery.

3. Clock Tower (sahat Kula):
The Clock Tower, also known as Sahat Kula, is a historical landmark that stands tall in the heart of Old Town. This Ottoman-era tower, dating from the

17th century, served as a timekeeper for the local community. With its distinct architectural style, the Clock Tower serves as a visible reminder of Podgorica's past. Visitors can climb to the top of the tower for panoramic views of the surrounding area, including Stara Varoš and the city center. Inside the tower, there is a small museum that showcases Podgorica's history.

4. King Nikola's Palace:

King Nikola's Palace is a magnificent residence located near the city center. This neoclassical palace, built in the nineteenth century, was the royal residence of Montenegro's King Nikola I. Today, it serves as a museum for Montenegrin history and culture. The palace's elegant interiors feature period furniture, artwork, and historical artifacts. Visitors can tour the palace's various rooms, which include the king's study, reception halls, and the royal chapel. The surrounding gardens offer a peaceful respite and a glimpse into the royal lifestyle of the past.

5. The Natural History Museum of Montenegro:

The Natural History Museum of Montenegro is a must-see for nature lovers and anyone interested in the region's biodiversity. Located in the city center, the museum houses a large collection of exhibits showcasing Montenegro's diverse flora and fauna. Visitors can look through displays of fossils, minerals, preserved animal specimens, and educational exhibits about the country's ecosystems. The museum also provides interactive activities and educational programs, making it an enjoyable visit for people of all ages.

6. Church of the Holy Heart of Jesus.

The Church of the Holy Heart of Jesus is a stunning Catholic church located in the city centre. This architectural gem combines Gothic and Romanesque styles, with intricate detailing and stained glass windows. The church's serene interior creates a tranquil setting for reflection and prayer. Visitors can admire the church's stunning architecture, religious artwork, and peaceful atmosphere.

These must-see landmarks and attractions in Podgorica City Center showcase the city's history, culture, and architectural heritage. Exploring these sites will help you understand Podgorica's past and present.

Recommendations for walking tours and guided excursions

1. Podgorica City Walking Tour: Take a guided walking tour of Podgorica to see the city's highlights while learning about its history and culture. A knowledgeable guide will lead you through the city center, explaining the landmarks, architecture, and local life. The tour may include stops at Podgorica City Hall, the Millennium Bridge, the Clock Tower, King Nikola's Palace, and other notable landmarks. You'll be able to immerse yourself in the city's atmosphere, ask questions, and discover hidden gems that you might not find on your own.

2. Old Town Stroll: Take a leisurely walk through Podgorica's charming Old Town and learn about its rich history. You'll follow a guide through narrow cobblestone streets lined with traditional stone houses, Ottoman-era buildings, and quaint shops. The guide will share stories about the history and cultural significance of the Old Town, highlighting landmarks like the Clock Tower, Osmanagić Mosque, Ribnica Fortress, and the remnants of the old city walls. This tour provides a glimpse into Podgorica's history while also allowing you to enjoy the authentic ambiance of the historic district.

3. Moraca River Promenade: Take a guided tour of the Moraca River promenade, a scenic pathway that winds along the riverbanks. This tranquil walkway, surrounded by greenery and scenic landscapes, provides a peaceful escape from the hustle and bustle of the city. Your guide will explain the significance of the river as well as the flora and fauna that surround it. The tour may also include visits to notable landmarks along the way, such as the Millennium Bridge, Temple of Christ's Resurrection, and the iconic Red Keep Tower. It's an excellent opportunity to reconnect with nature and appreciate the natural beauty of Podgorica.

4. *Gorica Hill Hike:* For outdoor enthusiasts, a guided hike up Gorica Hill is strongly advised. This hill, located near the city center, provides panoramic views of Podgorica and its surroundings. Accompanied by a knowledgeable guide, you'll walk through scenic trails, past lush vegetation, and arrive at the hilltop. From there, you can enjoy stunning views of the city, the Moraca River, and the distant mountains. The guide will provide information on the local flora and fauna, as well as the historical significance of Gorica Hill. It's a satisfying experience that combines nature, exercise, and breathtaking scenery.

5. *Skadar Lake Boat Tour:* Although not located in Podgorica, a guided boat tour of Skadar Lake is an excellent excursion option for nature enthusiasts. Skadar Lake, the Balkans' largest freshwater lake, is close to the city. A guided boat tour allows you to discover the lake's diverse ecosystems, observe a variety of bird species, and visit picturesque fishing villages. The knowledgeable guide will explain the

lake's biodiversity, cultural heritage, and local way of life. It is a fully immersive experience that highlights the region's natural beauty.

These recommendations for walking tours and guided excursions in Podgorica offer a variety of perspectives on the city, its surroundings, and its cultural and natural attractions. Whether you prefer exploring the city center, delving into the history of the Old Town, taking scenic river walks, hiking in nature, or visiting nearby destinations, there are options to suit your interests.

Insight into local culture, traditions, and festivals

1. Montenegrin Cuisine: Learning about the local cuisine is an excellent way to immerse yourself in Podgorica's culture. Montenegrin cuisine is influenced by a variety of Mediterranean, Balkan, and Ottoman flavors. Traditional dishes frequently include lamb, seafood, cheese, prosciutto, and vegetables. Popular dishes include Njeguški Steak, Kačamak (cornmeal dish), Kajmak (creamy dairy product), and different types of local cheese. Do not pass up the opportunity to sample local wines and rakija (fruit brandy).

2. Folklore and Traditional Music: Montenegrins are deeply connected to their folklore and traditional music. Traditional costumes, dances, and songs are still celebrated and performed at cultural gatherings and festivals. If you have the opportunity, attend a folk music concert or festival to witness the lively rhythms, intricate dance moves, and traditional costumes that represent Montenegro's cultural heritage.

3. Religious Festivals: Montenegro's religious landscape is diverse, with Orthodox Christianity being the dominant faith. Religious festivals are an important part of the local culture, and attending them provides insight into religious traditions and customs. Orthodox Christian holidays, such as Christmas and Easter, are commemorated through special church services, processions, and family gatherings. Make sure to check the local calendar for religious festivals and events taking place during your visit.

4. *Podgorica Cultural Summer:* The Podgorica Cultural Summer is an annual festival held during the summer months that features a diverse range of cultural events, performances, and exhibitions. The festival features theater plays, music concerts, art exhibitions, film screenings, and dance performances, among other artistic expressions. It's a fantastic opportunity to get involved with the local arts scene, see live performances, and celebrate the city's cultural diversity.

5. *Independence Day:* Montenegro celebrates Independence Day on May 21st. This national holiday commemorates Montenegro's independence referendum, held on May 21, 2006. Official ceremonies, parades, concerts, and fireworks are all part of the festivities. It is a special day for

Montenegrins, and you can see the people's patriotic spirit and pride during the celebrations.

6. City Events and Exhibitions: Every year, Podgorica hosts a variety of exhibitions, cultural events, and art shows. These events allow local artists, craftspeople, and performers to showcase their talents. Keep an eye out for art exhibitions, photography displays, theater performances, and other cultural events throughout the city. Attending these events allows you to connect with the local art scene and gain a better understanding of Podgorica's cultural landscape.

You can learn about Podgorica's culture, traditions, and way of life by sampling local cuisine, attending folk music events, taking part in religious festivals, and attending cultural celebrations.

CHAPTER 4:

CULTURAL AND HISTORICAL SITES

Key Historical Sites in Podgorica

Podgorica Citadel:

The Podgorica Citadel, also known as the Castle of King Nicholas, is an important historical site in the heart of Podgorica. This fortress dates back to the Roman era and has been rebuilt several times throughout its history. It served as a strategic stronghold at various times, including the Ottoman and Austro-Hungarian occupations.

The Citadel's architecture is a mix of styles, reflecting the influences of various ruling powers. The fortress contains remnants of ancient walls, towers, and a central courtyard. The fortress provides a panoramic view of the city and surrounding landscape. It's a fascinating place to explore, with its historical atmosphere and remnants of previous civilizations.

Ribnica Fortress:

The Ribnica Fortress, located on the banks of the Ribnica River, is another significant historical site in Podgorica. This medieval fortress, built in the 15th century, played an important role in defending the city from invasions. The fortress was strategically placed to control the routes into Podgorica and protect its inhabitants.

The Ribnica Fortress features well-preserved stone walls, towers, and a central keep. Exploring the fortress allows you to imagine its former glory and appreciate its architectural and defensive features. From the top of the fortress, you'll have commanding views of the river, the city, and the surrounding countryside. The site provides insight into

Podgorica's medieval past and its strategic importance throughout history.

King Nikola's Palace:

King Nikola's Palace is an elegant neoclassical residence located near Podgorica's city center. The palace, built in the late nineteenth century, was the royal residence of Montenegro's King Nikola I and his family. It commemorates a pivotal period in Montenegrin history, when the country was a monarchy.

The palace has stunning architectural features, such as decorative facades, ornate interiors, and beautiful gardens. Inside, you will find well-preserved rooms that reflect the royal family's opulent lifestyle. The palace now serves as a museum, with visitors able to explore the living quarters, reception halls, and royal chapel. The museum exhibits historical artifacts, artwork, and personal belongings of the royal family, providing insight into Montenegro's monarchical period.

Clock Towers:

The Clock Tower is a prominent landmark in the heart of Podgorica. This historic tower, dating back to the Ottoman era, serves as a symbol of the city's past. It was once part of a mosque complex but was later converted into a clock tower. The tower provides a glimpse into Podgorica's Ottoman heritage and panoramic views of the surrounding area from its top.

Orthodox Cathedral of the Resurrection of Christ.

The Orthodox Cathedral of the Resurrection of Christ is a magnificent religious building in Podgorica. This grand cathedral, built in the early twentieth century, is influenced by Byzantine architectural styles. It is Montenegro's largest Orthodox church and the seat of the Montenegrin Metropolitanate and Littoral. The cathedral's interior boasts stunning frescoes and iconography, while the exterior is embellished with intricate detailing and decorative elements.

Memorial House of King Nikola:

The Memorial House of King Nikola is a museum dedicated to Montenegrin King Nikola I, located in Njegusi (about 30 kilometers from Podgorica). King Nikola I was a pivotal figure in Montenegrin history, guiding the country through its independence and subsequent periods. The museum displays personal belongings, photographs, documents, and exhibits about the king and his family. Visiting the Memorial House provides insight into the life and legacy of this powerful ruler.

Roman mosaics at the Duklja Archaeological Site:

The Duklja Archaeological Site, near Podgorica, is home to well-preserved Roman mosaics from the fourth and fifth centuries. These ancient mosaics, which once adorned a Roman villa complex, depict intricate geometric patterns, mythical creatures, and scenes from everyday life. Exploring the site allows you to witness the Roman craftsmen's skill and artistry while also providing a fascinating glimpse into the region's Roman history.

Visiting key historical sites such as the Podgorica Citadel, Ribnica Fortress, and King Nikola's Palace allows you to learn about Podgorica and Montenegro's rich history. These sites provide glimpses into various eras, including ancient times, the medieval period, and the more recent monarchy. Exploring their architectural features, learning about their historical significance, and appreciating the cultural heritage they represent all contribute to a better understanding of the city's history.

Museums, galleries, and cultural institutions to visit

1. National Museum of Montenegro:

The National Museum of Montenegro is a prominent cultural institution in Podgorica. It consists of several buildings, including the Museum of History, the Museum of Art, the Archaeological Museum, the Ethnographic Museum, and the King Nikola Museum. The museum complex houses a large collection of artifacts, artworks, historical objects, and archaeological findings that shed light on Montenegro's history, art, and cultural heritage.

2. The Contemporary Art Center of Montenegro

The Contemporary Art Center of Montenegro serves as a hub for contemporary art exhibitions and events. It hosts rotating exhibitions of works by local and international artists in a variety of artistic mediums, including painting, sculpture, photography, video art, and installation. The center's mission is to promote contemporary art, encourage artistic dialogue, and engage the public in cultural activities.

3. The Millennium Bridge Gallery:

The Millennium Bridge Gallery, located near the Millennium Bridge, promotes contemporary art in Podgorica. It hosts regular art exhibitions featuring the works of both local and international artists. The gallery showcases emerging artists and promotes artistic expression and creativity.

4. The Petrovic Palace Art Museum:

The Petrovic Palace, located in the city center, houses the Art Museum. The museum houses a diverse collection of artworks, including paintings, sculptures, and installations by Montenegrin and international artists. The Petrovic Palace is an architectural masterpiece that combines neoclassical and baroque styles. Exploring the museum allows you to appreciate the palace's historical significance as well as its artistic creations.

5. Montenegro National Theater:

The Montenegrin National Theatre is Podgorica's premier performing arts institution. It hosts a wide range of theatrical performances, including dramas, comedies, operas, and ballet. Attending a show at the National Theater allows you to experience Montenegrin performing arts and see the talents of local actors, dancers, and musicians.

6. *The Natural History Museum of Montenegro*

The Natural History Museum of Montenegro is a must-see for anyone interested in natural history. The museum houses a diverse collection of exhibits related to the country's flora, fauna, geology, and paleontology. The museum offers an educational and immersive experience, featuring fossils and mineral specimens as well as taxidermy displays and educational exhibits.

These museums, galleries, and cultural institutions provide a wide range of artistic and cultural experiences in Podgorica. Whether you're interested in history, art, theater, or natural sciences, these venues allow you to discover and appreciate the city's vibrant cultural scene.

CHAPTER 5:

NATURAL BEAUTY AND OUTDOOR ACTIVITIES

Overview of the Surrounding Natural Landscapes

Nestled in the heart of Montenegro, Podgorica is surrounded by breathtaking natural landscapes that beckon outdoor enthusiasts and nature lovers. From the tranquil shores of Lake Skadar to the imposing Moraca River Canyon and the scenic Gorica Hill, the region offers a diverse range of natural beauty to explore.

Lake Skadar, the largest lake in the Balkans, is a pristine oasis located near Podgorica. Lake Skadar, with its crystal-clear waters, lush wetlands, and picturesque islands, is a birdwatcher, kayaker, and nature lover's paradise. Exploring the lake by boat allows you to discover hidden coves, see a variety of bird species, and relax in the tranquility of this natural wonder. The surrounding villages provide an insight into traditional Montenegrin life, and sampling local cuisine is a must-do activity.

The Moraca River Canyon, northeast of Podgorica, is a breathtaking natural wonder characterized by steep cliffs, rugged terrain, and the roaring Moraca River. The canyon provides thrilling opportunities for hiking, rock climbing, and river rafting, allowing adventurers to experience the raw beauty and adrenaline-inducing challenges of Montenegro's wilderness. As you travel the scenic trails and navigate the river's rapids, you'll be rewarded with breathtaking views and a strong sense of connection to nature.

Gorica Hill, located in the heart of Podgorica, offers a peaceful escape within city limits. This green oasis has well-kept paths for walking, jogging, and cycling, making it a popular destination for outdoor activities and leisurely walks. The hill's summit offers panoramic views of the city, surrounding mountains, and the confluence of the Ribnica and Moraca rivers. Gorica Hill's tranquil ambiance and lush vegetation make it an ideal place to unwind and reconnect with nature right in the heart of town.

Insider Tip: To get an authentic experience, consider taking a guided tour or excursion to explore these natural landscapes. Local guides can provide useful information, tell fascinating stories, and take you to hidden gems off the beaten path. In addition, check the weather and pack appropriate gear and supplies, especially for activities like hiking or kayaking. Respecting the environment and leaving no trace when visiting these natural wonders is critical to preserving their beauty for future generations.

These natural landscapes surrounding Podgorica provide numerous outdoor activities as well as the opportunity to immerse yourself in Montenegro's breathtaking beauty. From tranquil lakeshores to rugged canyons and verdant hills, the region's natural wonders beckon exploration and provide unforgettable experiences for nature lovers and adventurers alike.

Hiking, Biking, and Adventure Sports Opportunities

Podgorica and its surrounding natural landscapes offer an abundance of opportunities for outdoor enthusiasts seeking hiking, biking, and adventure sports experiences. With its diverse terrain, rugged mountains, and pristine trails, the region caters to both novice adventurers and seasoned thrill-seekers.

Hiking in Montenegro is a truly rewarding experience, and Podgorica is an excellent starting point for exploring the country's stunning trails. The nearby mountains, including the Durmitor, Prokletije, and Bjelasica ranges, provide a variety of hiking routes suitable for all skill levels. Whether you're climbing a mountain peak or walking through scenic valleys, you'll be rewarded with breathtaking views, alpine meadows, cascading waterfalls, and the opportunity to see rare wildlife. Popular hiking trails near Podgorica include the Vranjina-Mratinje Trail, the Rikavac Waterfall Trail, and the Komovi Mountain Circuit.

Bikers will find plenty to enjoy in and around Podgorica. The city itself has an expanding network of bike lanes, making it simple to explore its urban areas on two wheels. For more daring biking adventures, the surrounding mountains and countryside provide thrilling off-road trails and scenic routes. The rugged terrain and picturesque landscapes make for an ideal mountain biking destination, with trails ranging from easy rides along Lake Skadar's shores to challenging ascents in Durmitor National Park. Biking through the Montenegrin countryside allows you to reconnect with nature, discover hidden villages, and enjoy the freedom of exploration on two wheels.

Podgorica and its surroundings provide a variety of exciting activities for adrenaline junkies. The Moraca River, with its rapids and gorges, offers an exciting setting for white-water rafting and kayaking. Experienced guides can lead you through the river's twists and turns, ensuring your safety while also providing excitement. The region also provides opportunities for canyoning, rock climbing, and paragliding, allowing you to push your limits and enjoy the thrill of these adrenaline-fueled activities.

Insider Tip: Before participating in any adventure sports activities, choose reputable tour operators or guides who prioritize safety and follow professional standards. They can provide the necessary equipment, instruction, and guidance to ensure a memorable experience while reducing risks. It's also a good idea to check the weather, pack appropriate gear, and notify others of your plans before venturing into the mountains or engaging in more remote activities.

Whether you're hiking to majestic peaks, biking through picturesque landscapes, or participating in thrilling adventure sports, Podgorica and its surroundings provide an ideal playground for outdoor enthusiasts. Embrace the spirit of exploration, immerse yourself in Montenegro's natural beauty, and make memories to last a lifetime.

National parks and protected areas worth exploring

Montenegro is home to several national parks and protected areas that showcase the country's stunning natural beauty. Here are some national parks and protected areas near Podgorica that are worth exploring:

1. Durmitor National Park: Located in northern Montenegro, Durmitor National Park is a UNESCO

World Heritage Site known for its breathtaking mountain scenery. The park includes the Tara River Canyon, Europe's deepest canyon, as well as glacial lakes, rugged peaks, dense forests, and alpine meadows. Popular activities in this pristine wilderness include hiking, mountain biking, rafting, and wildlife spotting.

2. Biogradska Gora National Park: Located in central Montenegro, Biogradska Gora National Park is known for its untouched forest and Biogradsko Lake, which is one of Europe's last three primeval forests. The park has a number of hiking trails, including one around the lake, where you can enjoy nature's tranquility while observing a variety of plant and animal species.

3. Skadar Lake National Park: Skadar Lake National Park, located southwest of Podgorica, is the Balkans' largest lake and a haven for birdwatchers and nature lovers. The park preserves the lake's diverse ecosystem, which includes wetlands, marshes, and floating vegetation. Take a boat tour to see the lake, charming fishing villages, and a variety of bird species, including the rare Dalmatian pelican.

4. *Lovćen National Park,* located in the rugged mountains near the Bay of Kotor, is a natural and historical treasure. Mount Lovćen, located in the park, provides stunning panoramic views of the surroundings. Explore the park's hiking trails, visit the famous Njegoš Mausoleum atop Jezerski Vrh, and learn about Montenegro's rich cultural heritage.

5. *Prokletije National Park:* Situated in the southeastern part of Montenegro, Prokletije National Park is a wilderness paradise with rugged peaks, deep canyons, glacial lakes, and dense forests. It is part of the Balkan Mountain Range, also known as the "Accursed Mountains." Hikers and mountaineers will find numerous challenging trails, while nature

lovers will be enthralled by the park's pristine beauty and diverse flora and fauna.

Insider Advice: When visiting national parks and protected areas, it is critical to follow the rules and regulations in place to protect the natural environment. Follow designated trails, avoid littering, and do not disturb wildlife. Consider visiting these parks on weekdays or outside of peak tourist seasons for a more tranquil and immersive experience.

Exploring Montenegro's national parks and protected areas allows you to reconnect with nature, see breathtaking scenery, and appreciate the country's diverse wildlife. Whether you're looking for outdoor adventures, peaceful hikes, or wildlife encounters, these natural treasures provide unforgettable experiences for nature lovers and adventurers alike.

CHAPTER 6:

DINING AND LOCAL CUISINE

Introduction to Montenegrin Cuisine and Regional Specialties

When visiting Podgorica, it's impossible to fully appreciate the city without sampling the rich and diverse Montenegrin cuisine. Montenegrin cuisine is influenced by its geographical location and neighboring countries, with flavors from the Mediterranean, Balkans, and Central Europe. Podgorica, the capital city, has a diverse range of dining options, from traditional taverns to upscale restaurants serving authentic dishes and regional specialties.

1. Meat Delights: Montenegrins have a strong appreciation for meat, and their cuisine reflects this. Try the regional specialty "ćevapi" - small grilled minced meat sausages served with warm bread, onions, and creamy kaymak cheese. "Raštan" is a popular dish that combines pickled cabbage, meat cuts, and spices. For a one-of-a-kind culinary experience, try "priganice" - deep-fried dough balls often served with honey or cheese, which make an excellent snack or dessert.

2. *Seafood Delicacies:* Despite being a landlocked city, Podgorica benefits from Montenegro's proximity to the Adriatic Sea, which allows for a delectable variety of seafood options. Fresh fish, such as sea bream, sea bass, and mackerel, are typically grilled and served with a drizzle of olive oil, lemon, and herbs. "Brodet" is a fisherman's stew that combines various types of fish, onions, tomatoes, and garlic to make a rich and flavorful dish. Don't miss out on trying "black risotto," a unique delicacy made

with cuttlefish ink and rice that has a striking black color and a savory flavor.

3. Dairy Delights: Montenegrin cuisine features an abundance of dairy products. The country is known for its high-quality cheeses, particularly "njeguški sir" which is a semi-hard, smoked cheese with a distinctive flavor. It pairs well with locally sourced prosciutto. Another cheese to try is "kajmak" - a creamy and tangy dairy product that pairs well with bread, meat, or vegetables.

4. Vegetable Delicacies: Montenegrin cuisine offers a wide range of vegetable-based dishes for vegetarians and vegans alike. "Uštipci" are deep-fried dough balls containing grated zucchini, potatoes, or pumpkin, providing a flavorful and satisfying option. "Kačamak" is a traditional cornmeal dish served with cheese, yogurt, or sour cream for a hearty and comforting meal. Fresh salads with locally sourced ingredients, such as tomatoes, cucumbers, and peppers, are also popular as side dishes or appetizers.

5. Sweet Temptations: **No** culinary journey to Montenegro is complete without trying the country's sweets. "Palačinke" are thin pancakes with fillings like Nutella, jam, and cheese. "Krofne" are fluffy donuts stuffed with chocolate or fruit jam. Enjoy "priganice" deep-fried dough balls dusted with powdered sugar and served with honey. Try "kacamak sa pavlakom" (warm cornmeal dessert with sour cream and honey) for a truly decadent experience.

Insider Tip: When dining in Podgorica, visit the city's traditional taverns known as "konobas" or "kafanas." These establishments provide an authentic atmosphere and the opportunity to savor traditional dishes while listening to live music or traditional folk performances.

Podgorica's dining scene offers a diverse range of culinary delights, including hearty meat dishes, fresh seafood, and dairy products. Exploring the city's local cuisine will undoubtedly improve your travel experience and give you a better understanding of Montenegrin culture.

Recommendations Best Restaurants and Hotels In Podgorica and What to Eat.

1. Pod Volat: Located in the heart of Podgorica, Pod Volat is a popular restaurant known for its warm and rustic atmosphere. The menu features a variety of traditional Montenegrin dishes, including grilled meats, seafood, and vegetarian options. Don't miss their signature dish, "Volat steak," which is a succulent grilled steak served with roasted potatoes and a variety of homemade sauces.

2. Murano Restaurant: Murano Restaurant, located along the Moraca River, combines a beautiful setting with a delicious menu. This upscale restaurant specializes in Mediterranean and Italian cuisine, serving a variety of seafood and homemade pastas. Try their seafood risotto or the grilled octopus, both made with fresh ingredients and packed with flavor.

3. Pod Volat 2: Pod Volat 2, a sister restaurant to the original Pod Volat, serves a similar menu with a modern twist. The restaurant's contemporary interior and outdoor terrace provide a chic setting for sampling Montenegrin cuisine. The "ćevapi" platter features grilled meat sausages, kaymak cheese, ajvar (roasted red pepper spread), and fresh bread.

4. *Lake Lounge Restaurant:* For an unforgettable dining experience, visit Lake Lounge Restaurant, which is located near Lake Moraca. This restaurant has stunning lake views and a relaxing atmosphere. Their menu combines Mediterranean and international cuisine, including grilled sea bass, lamb chops, and vegetarian options. To complete the dining experience, pair your meal with a selection of Montenegrin wines.

5. *Hemingway Bar & Restaurant:* Located in the city center, Hemingway Bar & Restaurant is a trendy

establishment known for its lively atmosphere and innovative cuisine. Their menu blends Montenegrin flavors with international influences, featuring beef tenderloin medallions, grilled salmon, and gourmet burgers. Save room for their delectable desserts, such as chocolate lava cake and homemade ice cream.

Restaurants:

1. Pod Volat Green Market: Located near the city's main green market, this restaurant uses fresh, locally sourced ingredients. Enjoy traditional Montenegrin dishes such as "njeguški sir" (smoked cheese), prosciutto, and grilled meats. The cozy and rustic ambiance enhances the dining experience.

2. Restoran Most: Located near the Millennium Bridge, Restoran Most boasts a breathtaking view of the Moraca River. The menu combines Mediterranean and Montenegrin cuisine, with a focus on seafood specialties. Try their seafood platter, which features a variety of grilled fish and shellfish.

Hotels with Local Delights:

1. Hilton Podgorica Crna Gora: This luxurious hotel's two renowned restaurants, Skybar and Restaurant Crna Gora, provide an unforgettable dining experience. Sample traditional Montenegrin dishes with a modern twist, as well as international cuisine. The hotel's central location makes it easy to explore the city's attractions.

2. Hotel M: Located in the city center, Hotel M features a restaurant specializing in Montenegrin cuisine. Enjoy a wide range of meat and seafood dishes, as well as vegetarian options. The hotel's comfortable rooms and friendly staff make it an excellent choice for travelers looking for local delights.

3. Hotel Hemera: Located in a quiet neighborhood near the city center, Hotel Hemera features a restaurant that serves a mix of international and Montenegrin cuisine. Experience the flavors of local cuisine with their carefully crafted menu, which includes both meat and vegetarian options. The hotel's modern design and cozy atmosphere ensure a comfortable stay.

Insider Tip: Montenegro has a vibrant wine culture, so don't pass up the opportunity to pair your meal with local wines. Ask the restaurant staff for suggestions on the best wine pairings to enhance your dining experience.

These Podgorica restaurants serve a variety of culinary delights, including traditional Montenegrin dishes and international flavors. Exploring these establishments will allow you to enjoy the city's vibrant dining scene while also discovering Montenegro's diverse flavors.

Vegetarian and vegan options

1. Green Market: Located in the city center, Podgorica's Green Market is a haven for fresh produce and local delicacies. Explore the market and find a wide variety of fruits, vegetables, herbs, and nuts. You can buy ingredients to make your own vegetarian or vegan meals, or you can eat seasonal produce such as juicy tomatoes, crisp cucumbers, and flavorful olives.

2. Lovac Restaurant: Lovac Restaurant, known for its traditional Montenegrin cuisine, also serves vegetarian and vegan options. Begin with "uštipci," a popular deep-fried dough ball made from grated zucchini or pumpkin. Their menu features stuffed peppers with rice and vegetables, grilled vegetables with polenta, and fresh salads made with locally sourced ingredients.

3. *Veggies Fast Food:* A vegetarian and vegan restaurant in Podgorica. They serve a variety of plant-based options, such as vegan burgers, falafel wraps, vegetable stir-fries, and salads. Their menu focuses on healthy, sustainable, and delicious vegetarian and vegan options, allowing you to have a satisfying meal while adhering to your dietary preferences.

4. *Hotel Hemera:* Hotel Hemera, which was previously mentioned for its local delights, also serves vegetarian and vegan cuisine. Vegetarian options on the menu include vegetable risotto, grilled vegetables, and pasta. The culinary team is accommodating and can modify dishes to meet specific dietary requirements.

5. *Hotel M:* Another recommended hotel, Hotel M, has a vegetarian and vegan menu in its restaurant. The menu includes dishes such as vegetable stir-fries, risottos, and salads made with local ingredients. The staff is attentive and will assist you in finding suitable vegetarian or vegan options.

Insider Tip: When dining out, make your dietary preferences clear to the restaurant staff. They are frequently accommodating and can suggest changes or create customized dishes to meet your specific requirements. Additionally, don't be afraid to ask about the ingredients and cooking methods used to ensure that your meal meets your dietary requirements.

Podgorica is seeing an increase in the number of vegetarian and vegan dining options, ranging from restaurants with dedicated menus to hotels that provide suitable alternatives. Exploring these establishments will allow you to savor local flavors while enjoying a plant-based meal.

Famous Local Drinks To Try in Podgorica.

When visiting Podgorica, there are several famous local drinks that you should try to experience the flavors of Montenegro. Here are a few popular local drinks in Podgorica:

1. Rakija: Rakija is a traditional fruit brandy with strong cultural and social significance in Montenegro. It is typically made with a variety of fruits, including plums, grapes, and apples. Rakija is frequently served as a welcome drink or as a symbol of hospitality. It has a strong and distinct flavor and is best consumed in moderation.

2. Vranac: A red wine grape variety native to Montenegro. It produces full-bodied red wines with flavors of dark fruits and spices. Vranac wines are highly regarded and play an important role in Montenegrin winemaking tradition. When in Podgorica, you can sample various Vranac wines and learn about the local wine culture.

3. *Nikšićko Pivo*: A popular local beer made in Nikšić, a town near Podgorica. It is considered Montenegro's national beer and is widely consumed across the country. Nikšićko Pivo is a refreshing lager with a smooth flavor. It can be found in a variety of bars, restaurants, and supermarkets throughout Podgorica.

4. *Kruškovac:* This sweet pear liqueur is commonly served as an aperitif or digestif. It is made from ripe pears and infused with spices and herbs, producing a flavorful and aromatic beverage. Kruškovac is a great

option for those who enjoy sweeter, fruit-based liqueurs.

5. Nektar: Nektar is a popular soft drink in Montenegro, available in a variety of flavors including orange, lemon, and grapefruit. It is a carbonated beverage with a refreshing, fruity flavor. Nektar is widely available in Podgorica and is an excellent non-alcoholic beverage to quench your thirst.

These are just a few of the well-known local beverages you can sample while visiting Podgorica. They provide a taste of Montenegrin culture and traditions, allowing you to immerse yourself in regional flavors and beverages.

Tips on trying regional beverages and wines

1. Research Local Specialties: Prior to your trip, spend some time researching the regional beverages and wines of the area you will be visiting. Learn about traditional winemaking techniques, grape varieties, and flavor profiles. This will give you a better idea of what to expect and allow you to enjoy the drinks more.

2. Visit Local Wineries and Breweries: Visiting local wineries and breweries is a great way to get a taste of regional beverages. Take guided tours, taste the drinks, and learn about the production process from the experts. It's an excellent opportunity to immerse yourself in the local beverage culture and learn from the people who make them.

3. Seek Recommendations: Ask locals, hotel staff, or knowledgeable experts for suggestions on the best regional beverages and wines to sample. They can offer useful insights and recommendations based on your preferences. Don't be afraid to ask for their advice and opinions to help you make informed decisions.

4. Sample a Variety: When trying regional beverages, it's best to try a variety of options. Explore the region's various styles, flavors, and brands. This allows you to expand your tastes and find new favorites. To get a full taste of the region's offerings, try both popular and lesser-known options.

5. Consider Food Pairings: Regional beverages often complement local cuisine. Consider pairing traditional foods with the drinks to enhance the flavors and create a harmonious dining experience. Local dishes can complement and enhance the flavor of the beverages, resulting in a more authentic and enjoyable culinary adventure.

6. Take Notes: If you want to learn more about regional beverages and wines, consider taking notes while tasting. Take notes on your impressions, flavor profiles, and any unique characteristics you notice. This can help you remember your favorites and use them as a reference for future exploration.

7. Enjoy Responsibly: Remember to drink responsibly and stay within your limits. If you're sampling a variety of beverages or wines, take your time and enjoy each one. Stay hydrated and be aware of the alcohol content. When enjoying regional drinks, it is critical to prioritize your health and safety.

By following these guidelines, you can make the most of your experience sampling regional beverages and wines. It's a great way to connect with the local culture, sample unique flavors, and make lasting memories while traveling.

Chapter 7.

Where To Sleep.

Best Luxury Hotels in Podgorica.

Luxury Hotels:

1. Hilton Podgorica Crna Gora: Located in the city center, the Hilton Podgorica Crna Gora provides luxurious accommodations and a variety of amenities. The hotel has elegantly designed rooms, a spa and wellness center, a variety of dining options, and a rooftop terrace with breathtaking views. It is conveniently located near the city's attractions and offers a high standard of comfort and service.

2. Hotel Ramada Podgorica: Situated just outside of the city center, Hotel Ramada Podgorica provides a luxurious stay with modern amenities. The hotel features spacious rooms, a rooftop pool with a bar, a fitness center, and a restaurant that serves both international and local cuisine. It offers a peaceful atmosphere while remaining close to Podgorica's main attractions.

3. CentreVille Hotel & Experiences: Situated in the city center, the CentreVille Hotel provides modern and stylish accommodations. The hotel has comfortable rooms with contemporary designs, a rooftop terrace with panoramic views, a fitness center, and a restaurant that serves Mediterranean and international cuisine. It is renowned for its exceptional service and convenient location.

4. Hotel Aurel: A boutique hotel located near the Millennium Bridge. It features tastefully decorated rooms, a garden terrace, and a restaurant that serves a variety of Mediterranean and international cuisine. The hotel has a cozy and intimate atmosphere, making it an appealing option for a relaxing stay.

5. *Hotel Ziya:* Hotel Ziya is a luxury hotel in the heart of Podgorica. It features elegant rooms with modern amenities, a rooftop pool, a spa center, and a restaurant that serves a mix of Montenegrin and international cuisine. The hotel's central location provides convenient access to the city's attractions and vibrant nightlife.

6. *Hotel Alexandar Lux:* Hotel Alexandar Lux is a boutique hotel located in a quiet neighborhood close to the city center. The hotel features spacious and well-appointed rooms, a restaurant serving a variety of dishes, and a terrace with panoramic views of the city. It offers a peaceful retreat while remaining close to the main sights.

7. Hotel Podgorica is a historic establishment near the city's main square. It combines classic charm and modern amenities. The hotel has comfortable rooms, a restaurant with traditional Montenegrin cuisine, a bar, and a casino. It is known for its convenient location and friendly service.

Insider Tip: When booking accommodation, consider the location and proximity to the attractions and areas you plan to explore. Additionally, check for amenities that are important to you, such as parking, Wi-Fi, and breakfast options, to ensure a comfortable stay.

These recommendations provide a mix of luxury hotels and alternative accommodation options in Podgorica. Whether you prefer the lavish amenities of luxury hotels or the cozy charm of apartments and guesthouses, you can find suitable options to make your stay in Podgorica enjoyable.

Best Boutique Hotels in Podgorica.

1. Hotel Keto: A charming boutique hotel in the city center. It provides stylish, individually designed rooms with modern amenities. The hotel has a cozy lounge area, a garden terrace, and a restaurant serving international and Montenegrin cuisine. Hotel Keto offers a one-of-a-kind and intimate experience through personalized service and attention to detail.

2. Hotel New Star: Hotel New Star is a boutique hotel located in a quiet residential neighborhood of Podgorica. The hotel provides well-appointed rooms with elegant decor and convenient amenities. It has a rooftop terrace, a restaurant serving Mediterranean and international cuisine, and a friendly atmosphere. Hotel New Star offers a peaceful retreat while remaining conveniently located near the city center.

3. Hotel Hemera: As previously mentioned, Hotel Hemera is a boutique hotel that blends modern design with a cozy atmosphere. The hotel provides stylish rooms with modern furnishings and amenities. It includes a restaurant serving local cuisine, a bar, and a garden area. Hotel Hemera offers a boutique experience through its attention to detail and personalized service.

4. Hotel Alexandar Lux: Hotel Alexandar Lux, as previously mentioned, is a boutique hotel that combines comfort and style. The hotel has spacious and elegantly designed rooms, a restaurant with a wide range of dishes, and a terrace with panoramic views. Hotel Alexandar Lux guarantees a memorable stay thanks to its boutique charm and focus on guest satisfaction.

5. *Hotel BaMBiS:* Hotel BaMBiS is a boutique hotel situated in a quiet neighborhood near the city center. The hotel's rooms are uniquely designed, combining modern and rustic elements. It has a garden terrace, a restaurant that serves traditional Montenegrin cuisine, and a friendly and welcoming atmosphere. Hotel BaMBiS offers a boutique experience through its distinct character and personalized service.

These boutique hotels in Podgorica offer a more intimate and distinctive lodging experience. From stylish design to personalized service, they provide a delightful and memorable stay in the city.

Budget Friendly Hotels, Hostels and Lodges In Podgorica.

1. Hotel Evropa: Hotel Evropa is a low-cost hotel located in the city center. It provides comfortable rooms with basic amenities at affordable prices. The hotel's convenient location allows for easy access to Podgorica's attractions, restaurants, and shops.

2. Hotel Laguna: Hotel Laguna is a budget hotel located near the city center. It provides simple and clean rooms with essential amenities. The hotel offers a 24-hour front desk, free Wi-Fi, and a restaurant serving affordable meals.

3. Hotel Crnogorska Kuća: Conveniently located in the city center, this hotel provides affordable accommodations. The rooms are clean and comfortable, and the hotel offers basic amenities like complimentary Wi-Fi and a 24-hour front desk. It's an excellent choice for budget-conscious travellers looking for a central location to stay.

4. Hotel Philia: Located near the city center, Hotel Philia provides affordable rooms with a cozy and welcoming atmosphere. The rooms are simple but comfortable, and the hotel offers amenities like free Wi-Fi and continental breakfast. The staff is friendly and accommodating, which makes it a popular choice for budget travelers.

5. Hostel Podgorica: Located in the city center, Hostel Podgorica provides affordable dormitory-style accommodations. The hostel offers clean and comfortable beds, a shared kitchen, a common area, and free Wi-Fi. It's an excellent choice for backpackers and budget travelers seeking a social and affordable place to stay.

6. Montenegro Hostel B&B Podgorica: Located near the city center, Montenegro Hostel B&B Podgorica provides affordable accommodations in a welcoming and relaxed environment. The hostel offers both dormitory-style and private rooms, as well as amenities like a communal kitchen, a common area, and complimentary Wi-Fi. The employees are known for their friendliness and helpfulness.

7. Apartments Athos: If you prefer self-catering, Apartments Athos provides affordable apartments with kitchenettes and basic amenities. The apartments are clean, comfortable, and conveniently located close to the city center. They are a cost-effective option for travelers who prefer more privacy and the freedom to cook their own meals.

8. Hotel M: Located in the city center, Hotel M provides affordable rooms with simple but comfortable furnishings. The hotel offers free Wi-Fi, a 24-hour front desk, and a bar where guests can unwind and have a drink. It's an ideal choice for budget travelers looking for a central location.

9. Hostel Podgorica-Niksic Road: Located near the main road connecting Podgorica and Niksic, this hostel provides affordable lodging for travelers passing through or exploring the surrounding area. The hostel has clean dormitory-style rooms, a shared kitchen, and a comfortable common area. It's an excellent choice for those on a tight budget who require easy access to transportation.

10. Apartment City Break: If you prefer a private apartment, Apartment City Break provides affordable lodging with kitchenettes and modern amenities. The apartments are near the city center and offer a comfortable and affordable place to stay. They are ideal for budget-conscious travelers or families seeking the convenience of a self-contained space.

11. Hostel Podgorica Center: Located in the city center, Hostel Podgorica Center provides affordable dormitory-style and private rooms. The hostel offers a communal kitchen, a common area, free Wi-Fi, and a welcoming environment. It's a popular choice for backpackers and solo travelers looking for affordable lodging in a central location.

12. Hotel Laguna: Located near the city center, Hotel Laguna provides affordable rooms with basic amenities. The hotel has a bar, a restaurant, and free WiFi. It offers a comfortable and reasonably priced option for travelers looking for a convenient place to stay without breaking the bank.

These budget-friendly hotels, hostels, and lodgings in Podgorica provide comfortable accommodations at reasonable rates, making them ideal for budget-conscious travelers. They provide all of the amenities needed for a comfortable stay while allowing you to save money for other city excursions.

Lodges:

1. Eco Resort Cermeniza: Eco Resort Cermeniza is a low-cost lodge located on the outskirts of Podgorica. It provides wood cabins and rooms surrounded by nature. The lodge has a garden, terrace, and a restaurant that serves organic food. It's an excellent choice for those looking for a peaceful escape from the city center.

2. Country House Ljubovic is a low-cost lodge located in a quiet village near Podgorica. It provides cozy rooms in a traditional countryside setting. The lodge includes a garden, a terrace, and a shared kitchen. It's an excellent choice for budget-conscious travelers who want to experience Montenegro's rural charm.

These inexpensive hotels, hostels, and lodges in Podgorica provide affordable lodging options without sacrificing comfort and convenience. Whether you prefer a budget hotel in the city center or a hostel/lodge with a more rustic atmosphere, these suggestions cater to a variety of tastes and budgets.

CHAPTER 8

SHOPPING AND SOUVENIRS

Overview of Shopping Districts, Malls, and Markets in Podgorica

Shopping in Podgorica, Montenegro's capital city, offers a wide range of options, from modern malls to traditional markets. Whether you're looking for high-end fashion, local crafts, or one-of-a-kind souvenirs, there are numerous shopping districts, malls, and markets to visit. Here's a detailed overview of some of the most popular shopping areas in Podgorica:

1. Delta City Mall: Delta City Mall, located in the city center, is one of Podgorica's largest and most popular shopping destinations. It offers a diverse selection of international and local brands, including clothing, accessories, electronics, and home furnishings. The mall also includes a food court, cafes, and entertainment options, making it a one-stop shop for both shopping and leisure.

2. *Mall of Montenegro:* Another well-known shopping complex located in the city center. It houses a variety of stores, including fashion, cosmetics, electronics, and home furnishings. The mall also includes a supermarket, a multiplex cinema, and a variety of dining options, making it a one-stop shopping and entertainment destination.

3. *City Kvart:* City Kvart is a modern shopping complex close to the city center. It houses a variety of local and international brands, as well as cafes, restaurants, and a supermarket. City Kvart is known for its modern architecture and lively atmosphere,

making it a popular destination for both locals and visitors.

4. *Njegoševa Street* is a popular shopping district in Podgorica, featuring a variety of shops, boutiques, and cafes. You'll find a mix of local and international brands, as well as specialty stores selling clothing, shoes, accessories, and more. The street has a lively atmosphere and is a great place to explore and find unique treasures.

5. *Vaka Đurovića Street,* located in the city center, is renowned for its luxury boutiques and high-end fashion stores. Renowned international brands and designer labels can be found here, providing fashion enthusiasts with a sophisticated shopping experience.

6. *Tržnica, or Green Market,* offers traditional Montenegrin shopping. This bustling market, located near the city center, serves as a vibrant hub of activity. A diverse selection of fresh produce, local delicacies, spices, cheeses, honey, and other items are available here. The market is also a great place to meet locals and enjoy Podgorica's vibrant atmosphere.

7. Ribnica Market: Located on the banks of the Ribnica River, Ribnica Market is another popular market in Podgorica. It provides a wide range of products, including fresh fruits and vegetables, fish, meat, and dairy products. The market is known for its authentic and locally sourced products, which offer a glimpse into Montenegro's culinary traditions.

These are just a few of the most notable shopping districts, malls, and markets in Podgorica. Exploring these areas will provide you with a full shopping experience, whether you're looking for international brands, local crafts, or fresh produce. Don't forget to immerse yourself in the local culture and interact with the friendly shopkeepers and artisans who make Podgorica's shopping scene so vibrant.

Local products and handicrafts to look out for While Shopping in Podgorica

When exploring Podgorica's shopping scene, there are several local products and handicrafts that you should look out for. These items showcase the rich cultural heritage and traditions of Montenegro. Here are some recommendations:

1. Traditional Clothing and Accessories: Montenegrin traditional clothing, or "nosnja," is an important part of the country's cultural identity. Look for garments like the "gunj," a traditional sleeveless coat, or the "kaput," a wool cloak. In addition, you will find intricately embroidered blouses, vests, and handwoven belts. These garments make excellent souvenirs that are both unique and authentic.

2. Handmade Jewelry: Montenegro is renowned for its exquisite handcrafted jewelry. Look for pieces made of silver, gold, or filigree, a delicate metalworking technique that results in intricate and ornate designs. Filigree earrings, pendants, and bracelets are popular choices and make lovely and meaningful gifts.

3. Olive Oil: Montenegro has a long history of olive oil production. Look for locally produced extra virgin olive oil, which is known for its superior quality and distinct flavor. There are many different varieties and flavors available, each with its own distinct characteristics. Montenegrin olive oil makes a delicious and healthy souvenir to bring home.

4. Honey and Bee Products: Montenegro's diverse natural landscapes create ideal conditions for beekeeping. Look for locally produced honey, such as the well-known "crnogorski med" (Montenegrin honey), made by bees that feed on the country's abundant floral resources. Other bee products include beeswax candles, propolis, and royal jelly.

5. Woven Rugs and Carpets: Montenegrin artisans are skilled at weaving rugs and carpets. These pieces frequently incorporate colorful patterns and geometric designs inspired by traditional motifs. Handwoven rugs and carpets can add a touch of Montenegrin tradition to your home decor.

6. Pottery and Ceramics: Look for handmade pottery and ceramics that reflect Montenegro's artistic traditions. From intricately painted plates and bowls to decorative vases and ornaments, these pieces showcase the skill and creativity of local artisans.

7. Local Spirits and Liqueurs: Montenegro is well-known for producing traditional spirits and liqueurs. Look for "rakija," a fruit brandy made from plums, grapes, and quince. Another popular local beverage is "loza," which is a grape-based spirit. These beverages make excellent gifts to share with friends and family.

When looking for local products and handicrafts, go to traditional markets, artisan shops, and boutiques. You'll be able to interact with the artisans themselves, learn about their craft, and choose from a larger selection of authentic and locally made items. Remember to ask questions, admire the craftsmanship, and support the local artisans who help to preserve Montenegro's cultural heritage.

Tips for bargaining and finding unique souvenirs From Local's Perspective

1. Visit the Markets: Podgorica has vibrant markets, such as the Green Market and the Ribnica Market, where you can find a variety of local products and souvenirs. Take your time browsing the stalls, interacting with the vendors, and comparing prices before making a purchase. These markets are frequently great places for bargaining, so don't be afraid to ask for a better deal.

2. Interact with the Artisans: To find truly one-of-a-kind souvenirs, visit artisan shops and boutiques. Many local artisans and craftsmen have small workshops or shops in Podgorica. These places frequently sell handcrafted items that reflect Montenegro's authentic culture and traditions. Engage with the artisans, ask them about their craft, and admire their abilities. This personal connection can also lead to opportunities for bargaining or customizing items.

3. Don't Be Afraid to Bargain: Bargaining is a common practice in Montenegro, particularly in markets and smaller stores. When negotiating a price, be courteous, friendly, and respectful. Begin by offering a lower price than the one quoted, and be ready for a counteroffer. The key is to find a price that both you and the vendor can agree on. Remember that bargaining is a part of the local culture, so enjoy the experience and don't be afraid to try it.

4. Look for Handmade Items: Look for items that highlight Montenegro's traditional crafts, such as handwoven textiles, pottery, jewelry, and woodwork.

These distinctive handicrafts frequently feature intricate designs that reflect the region's cultural heritage. Choosing these items not only provides you with a one-of-a-kind souvenir, but also helps to support local artisans and preserve their traditional skills.

5. Explore Off-the-Beaten-Path Areas: While malls and popular shopping districts provide convenience and a wide range of options, don't overlook off-the-beaten-path areas. Explore the narrow streets and alleys to find hidden gems such as small boutiques, antique stores, and local markets, which may sell more authentic and less touristy souvenirs. These lesser-known locations frequently provide a more intimate and authentic shopping experience.

6. Ask the Locals: When it comes to finding one-of-a-kind souvenirs, Podgorica locals can be a great resource. Start conversations with residents, hotel staff, or tour guides and ask for recommendations on where to find the best local products. They may recommend lesser-known shops, markets, or artisans who create unique souvenirs.

7. Quality over Quantity: When looking for souvenirs, value quality over quantity. Instead of purchasing multiple generic items, look for a few high-quality pieces that truly capture the essence of Montenegro. These one-of-a-kind and well-crafted souvenirs will hold sentimental value and serve as lasting reminders of your visit to Podgorica.

8. Learn Basic Phrases in Montenegrin: While many people in Podgorica speak English, knowing a few basic phrases in the local language, Montenegrin, will help you connect with vendors and artisans. Greeting them with a simple "Dobar dan" (Good day) or expressing gratitude with "Hvala" (Thank you) demonstrates respect and can contribute to a more positive and welcoming bargaining environment.

9. Timing is Everything: Choosing the right time can help you find unique souvenirs and get better deals. Consider going to markets and shops earlier in the day, when vendors are setting up their stalls or stores have just opened. This way, you may receive more time and attention from the vendors, as well as a better chance of finding freshly stocked items or negotiating lower prices before the crowds arrive.

Remember that the process of finding unique souvenirs and bargaining is about more than just the purchase; it's also about the experience and connection to the local culture. Enjoy the journey, immerse yourself in the local atmosphere, and make lasting memories during your shopping trips in Podgorica.

Insider recommendations for hidden gems and boutique shops

If you're looking for hidden gems and boutique shops in Podgorica, here are a few insider tips to help you find unique and lesser-known places. These shops provide a more intimate and personalized shopping experience, allowing you to find one-of-a-kind items. Below are some insider recommendations:

1. Duklja Souvenir Shop: Situated near the Millennium Bridge, Duklja Souvenir Shop is a hidden gem that sells genuine Montenegrin handicrafts and souvenirs. Pottery, jewelry, textiles, and wooden crafts are examples of beautifully handcrafted items available here. The shop supports local artisans and provides a diverse selection of one-of-a-kind pieces that reflect Montenegrin traditions and culture.

2. Pod Volat: Located in the heart of Old Town, Pod Volat is a charming boutique that features the work of local designers and craftspeople. This boutique features a carefully curated selection of fashion, accessories, home decor, and art. From stylish clothing to handmade ceramics and artwork, Pod Volat is a hidden gem for unique and high-quality items.

3. Uliks Bookstore & Café: Located in the city center, Uliks Bookstore & Café is a comfortable and welcoming space. This boutique bookstore carries a diverse selection of books in various genres, including works by local authors and translations of Montenegrin literature. You can browse the shelves and enjoy a cup of coffee or tea. Uliks frequently hosts literary events, making it a haven for book enthusiasts.

4. Atelier Dado: Atelier Dado is an art gallery and boutique that showcases the work of established and emerging local artists. This hidden gem, located near the Ribnica River, features a diverse collection of art, including paintings, sculptures, ceramics, and mixed media. The gallery also sells one-of-a-kind artworks and limited-edition prints, making it an excellent place to support local talent while discovering distinctive artworks.

5. Underground Wine & Coffee Bar: Located in the basement of a building near the city center, Underground Wine & Coffee Bar is a cozy and atmospheric establishment. This hidden gem serves a variety of local and international wines, as well as specialty coffee. The bar's unique setting, with exposed brick walls and low lighting, creates an intimate atmosphere, making it ideal for unwinding and sipping a glass of wine or a cup of coffee.

Remember that finding hidden gems and boutique shops often entails venturing off the beaten path, seeking recommendations from locals, and being open to unexpected discoveries. By venturing outside of the main shopping districts, you can discover unique establishments that showcase the creativity and craftsmanship of Podgorica's artisans and designers.

CHAPTER 9:

NIGHTLIFE AND ENTERTAINMENT

Overview of nightlife options, including bars, clubs, and live music venues

Podgorica offers a vibrant nightlife scene, with a variety of options for those looking to enjoy a night out on the town. Whether you're interested in lively bars, energetic clubs, or live music venues, the city has something to cater to different tastes and preferences. Here's an overview of the nightlife options in Podgorica:

1. Bars and Lounges: Podgorica has numerous bars and lounges where you can socialize, relax, and drink a variety of beverages. The city has everything from trendy cocktail bars to casual pubs. Some popular options include Hemingway Bar, a stylish venue known for its creative cocktails and cozy atmosphere, and The Old Town Pub, a traditional pub with a diverse selection of beers and live sports screenings. Other notable bars include Sky View Bar, which is located on a high-rise building's rooftop, and Mint Bar, a trendy spot with a modern ambiance.

2. Clubs and Nightclubs: If you want to dance and enjoy late-night entertainment, Podgorica has a variety of clubs and nightclubs to choose from. These venues frequently have live DJs, energetic dance floors, and a lively atmosphere. Maximus, the city's most well-known nightclub, is a large and popular venue that features both local and international DJs as well as themed parties. Another notable club is Montenegro Royal Club, which is known for its sophisticated ambiance and high-quality music.

3. Live Music Venues: For music lovers, Podgorica has live music venues where you can see performances by local bands and musicians. The Montenegrin National Theatre (Crnogorsko Narodno Pozorište) hosts cultural events like concerts and theatrical performances. Additionally, Hard Rock Cafe Podgorica occasionally hosts live music nights featuring local and international artists from various genres.

4. Open-Air Venues: During the summer, Podgorica comes alive with open-air venues that provide a one-of-a-kind nightlife experience. Ada Bojana, a river island near Ulcinj, features beach clubs and bars with drinks, music, and a lively atmosphere. Similarly, Lake Skadar, the largest lake in the Balkan region, has floating bars and restaurants where you can unwind and enjoy the stunning scenery.

5. Karaoke and Pub Quizzes: Podgorica offers interactive and entertaining experiences, such as karaoke bars and pub quizzes. These activities are an enjoyable and engaging way to spend an evening with friends or meet new people.

It is important to note that the nightlife in Podgorica varies according to the day of the week and season. Weekends are typically busier, with more options available. It's also a good idea to check local event listings, social media platforms, or speak with locals to stay up to date on the city's latest happenings and special events.

Whether you want to spend a relaxing evening at a cozy bar, an energetic night of dancing in a club, or enjoy live music performances, Podgorica's nightlife scene has something for everyone, making for an exciting and memorable experience.

Best Bars and NightClubs in Podgorica

Best Bars:

1. Hemingway Bar:

Location: Bokeska Street, Podgorica

Hemingway Bar, located in the city center, is a renowned establishment known for its sophisticated ambiance and creative cocktails. The bar draws inspiration from the famous writer Ernest Hemingway, creating an atmosphere reminiscent of the literary cafes of the past. The dimly lit interior, vintage decor, and comfortable seating create a cozy and intimate setting. Hemingway Bar is most known for its expertly crafted cocktails, which range from classic favorites to unique creations. The bartenders are highly skilled and can recommend the perfect drink to suit your taste. The bar also offers a wide selection of premium spirits, wines, and beers, ensuring a memorable and refined drinking experience.

2. Mint Bar:

Location: Novaka Miloseva, Podgorica

Mint Bar is a trendy and modern establishment known for its lively atmosphere and unique cocktails. The bar's interior is sleek and stylish, with contemporary decor and a lively atmosphere. It frequently hosts local DJs and occasional live music events, creating a dynamic and energetic atmosphere. Mint Bar serves a diverse menu of cocktails, including both classic and inventive concoctions made with fresh ingredients and unique flavor combinations. The bar also serves a variety of spirits, beers, and non-alcoholic beverages to cater to different tastes. Mint Bar's modern vibe and exciting drinks make it a popular choice for those looking for a lively nightlife experience.

Best bars:

3. Skyview Bar:

Location: Njegoševa Street in Podgorica.

Sky View Bar, located on the rooftop of a high-rise building, provides stunning panoramic views of Podgorica. The bar offers a unique and memorable environment for drinking. The interior is stylishly designed with comfortable seating, resulting in a relaxed and sophisticated environment. Sky View Bar is well-known for its extensive selection of wines, spirits, and cocktails, allowing guests to enjoy their favorite beverages while admiring the breathtaking cityscape. The experienced bartenders can recommend the ideal drink to suit your tastes, and the attentive service ensures a memorable evening. Whether you prefer a glass of fine wine, a classic cocktail, or a refreshing beer, Sky View Bar offers a sophisticated and scenic setting in which to relax and socialize.

4. Old Town Pub:

Location: Njegoševa Street in Podgorica.

The Old Town Pub is located in the heart of the city and exudes the charm of a traditional pub. The cozy interior boasts rustic decor, wooden furnishings, and a welcoming atmosphere. The pub is popular with both locals and visitors, and it is well-known for its extensive beer selection. It serves a diverse selection of local and international beers, including craft beers and seasonal specialties. The Old Town Pub is a great place to unwind with friends, watch live sports on large screens, and have a casual drink. The friendly staff and laid-back atmosphere make it a welcoming environment for patrons looking for a true pub experience in Podgorica.

5. *Maximus:* Maximus is a popular nightclub in the center of Podgorica. It's known for its upbeat atmosphere, live music performances, and DJ sets. The club hosts various themed nights featuring electronic, pop, and R&B music. Maximus draws a diverse crowd, including both locals and tourists, making it an excellent place to dance and socialize.

2. *Montenegro Pub*: Montenegro Pub is a popular bar near the city center. It has a relaxed and welcoming atmosphere and a diverse selection of beers, cocktails, and spirits. The pub frequently hosts live music events and features a popular outdoor terrace. Montenegro Pub is popular with both locals and visitors looking for a casual and enjoyable night out.

6. *Niagara Club:* Niagara Club is a trendy nightclub located in the city center. It features a spacious dance floor, a modern interior, and cutting-edge sound and lighting systems. The club hosts a variety of events, including DJ nights and themed parties, to cater to different musical tastes. Niagara Club is a popular hangout for people who enjoy electronic and dance music.

7. *Jazz Club Podgorica:* This cozy venue celebrates jazz music. It hosts live jazz performances by local and international artists, resulting in a relaxed and intimate atmosphere. The club's drink menu includes a variety of wines, beers, and cocktails. Jazz fans will appreciate the relaxed atmosphere and the opportunity to hear live music in an intimate setting.

8. *Strudla Culture Club:* The Strudla Culture
Club is a one-of-a-kind artistic venue in Podgorica. It
includes a cafe, a gallery, and a performance space.
The club hosts a variety of cultural events, such as art
exhibitions, live music, theatrical performances, and
poetry readings. Strudla Culture Club is a hub for
artists and creatives, offering a vibrant and unique
nightlife experience.

9. *The Living Room Lounge & Dining:* This
stylish and upscale venue combines a lounge,
restaurant, and bar. It has a stylish interior,
comfortable seating, and a diverse menu of premium
drinks. The venue hosts live music performances, DJ
sets, and occasional themed parties, making it ideal
for a sophisticated night out.

10. The Podgorica Beer Fest is an annual beer festival held in Podgorica. It features a variety of local and international craft beers, allowing visitors to sample and experience different brews. The festival also includes live music performances, food stalls, and a lively atmosphere, making it a great event for beer lovers.

11. Havana Lounge: This Cuban-themed bar and lounge is well-known for its vibrant atmosphere and live Latin music. It serves a wide variety of rum-based cocktails, including mojitos and daiquiris, offering a taste of Cuba in Podgorica. The venue frequently hosts salsa nights and provides dance lessons, which contributes to the lively and energetic atmosphere.

12. Sky View Lounge Bar: Sky View Lounge Bar is located on the top floor of a high-rise building and offers panoramic views of Podgorica. It provides a sophisticated and modern setting, making it ideal for sipping cocktails while admiring the cityscape. The bar has both indoor and outdoor seating, providing a memorable and scenic nightlife experience.

13. Irish Pub Podgorica: This establishment brings a touch of Irish hospitality to the city. It has a warm and inviting atmosphere with a traditional Irish pub feel. The pub serves a wide variety of Irish whiskeys, beers, and pub food. Live music performances, pub quizzes, and sports screenings are all regular features at the Irish Pub.

14. Vinyl Bar: Vinyl Bar is a one-of-a-kind venue that caters to music fans and vinyl collectors. It has a retro and nostalgic vibe, with vinyl records lining the walls. The bar serves a diverse selection of drinks and frequently hosts DJ nights, during which vinyl DJs spin a variety of genres, resulting in a unique and enjoyable nightlife experience.

These additional bars, clubs, and nightlife options in Podgorica increase the variety and options for visitors looking for an entertaining and vibrant evening out in the city.

It is worth noting that the nightlife scene in Podgorica varies according to the day of the week and season. Some venues may host special events or themed nights on certain days. In addition, it's always a good idea to check the local listings or ask locals for the most recent information on events and hotspots.

Please keep in mind that opening hours, entrance policies, and venue popularity may change, so double-check the information before planning your night out in Podgorica.

Best restaurants:
1. Pod Volat:
Location: Slobode Street in Podgorica.
Pod Volat is a boutique restaurant in the city center of Podgorica. The restaurant provides a stylish setting with chic and contemporary decor. The interior is tastefully decorated, resulting in an elegant and welcoming atmosphere. Pod Volat is famous for its delicious cuisine, which combines international flavors with local influences. The menu offers a variety of dishes made with fresh, locally sourced ingredients. From seafood delicacies to succulent meats and vegetarian options, the restaurant caters to a variety of tastes. The skilled chefs create dishes that are beautifully presented, demonstrating both culinary expertise and creativity. Pod Volat also has an extensive wine list, with a variety of local and international wines to complement the dining

experience. With its refined ambiance, delectable cuisine, and attentive service, Pod Volat offers a unique dining experience in Podgorica.

2. Lorenco and Kakalamba:

Location: Njegoševa Street in Podgorica.

Lorenco & Kakalamba is a popular restaurant that serves a fusion of Mediterranean and international cuisine. The restaurant's interior is eclectic and vibrant, with colorful artwork and unique decor that creates a lively and joyful atmosphere. Lorenco & Kakalamba serves a creative and diverse menu featuring a fusion of flavors and culinary techniques. The dishes are expertly prepared with fresh and locally sourced ingredients, resulting in a delicious culinary experience. The menu offers a variety of choices, including seafood specialties, pasta dishes, grilled meats, and vegetarian options. Each dish is carefully prepared, combining flavors and textures to create an unforgettable dining experience. With its lively atmosphere, this is one of the best places to visit while in Podgorica.

Safety tips and popular areas for nightlife in Podgorica

1. Stick to well-lit and populated areas: When exploring the nightlife in Podgorica, it's important to stick to well-lit and populated areas. Avoid isolated or dimly lit streets, especially late at night. Stick to the main thoroughfares where there are more people around, as this can act as a deterrent to potential incidents.

2. Travel in groups: It's always safer to travel in groups when enjoying the nightlife in any city, including Podgorica. Going out with friends or in a group provides an extra layer of security and reduces the chances of being targeted by pickpockets or other criminals.

3. Keep an eye on your belongings: It's essential to keep a close eye on your belongings, such as wallets, purses, and mobile phones, especially in crowded places. Use bags or purses with secure closures and keep them close to your body. Avoid leaving valuables unattended on tables or bar counters.

4. Drink responsibly: While enjoying the vibrant nightlife, it's important to drink responsibly. Pace yourself and know your limits. Excessive drinking can impair judgment and make you more vulnerable to potential dangers. Be aware of your surroundings and make sure to arrange for a safe way to get back to your accommodation, such as a designated driver or a trusted taxi service.

5. Use reliable transportation: When moving around the city at night, use reliable and licensed transportation options. Opt for registered taxis or reputable ride-hailing services to ensure your safety. Avoid accepting rides from unmarked or unofficial vehicles.

Popular Areas for Nightlife in Podgorica:

1. Stara Varoš (Old Town): Stara Varoš is a popular area for nightlife in Podgorica. It is known for its charming cobblestone streets, historic buildings, and a variety of bars, restaurants, and cafes. The area comes alive at night, offering a vibrant atmosphere with live music, outdoor seating, and a wide range of culinary delights.

2. Njegoševa Street: Njegoševa Street is another bustling area for nightlife in Podgorica. It is lined with numerous bars, clubs, and restaurants, catering to different tastes and preferences. The street offers a lively ambiance, especially during weekends, with music venues and dance floors where you can enjoy live performances or dance the night away.

3. Delta City Shopping Mall: Delta City Shopping Mall is not only a popular destination for shopping and entertainment but also offers a vibrant nightlife scene. The mall features a variety of restaurants, cafes, and bars where you can relax, socialize, and enjoy a diverse range of cuisines and beverages.

4. Bokeska Street: Bokeska Street is known for its cozy bars and pubs, making it a popular choice for those seeking a more relaxed and intimate nightlife experience. The street offers a laid-back ambiance, with establishments that often host live music performances and provide a cozy setting to enjoy a few drinks with friends.

Remember to check for the latest information and recommendations regarding nightlife locations and safety from local authorities or trusted sources before visiting Podgorica.

CHAPTER 10.

BEST THINGS TO DO.

The Most Romantic Things To Do In Podgorica.

When it comes to romantic activities in Podgorica, there are several charming and memorable experiences that couples can enjoy together. Here are some of the best romantic things to do in Podgorica:

1. Stroll along the Millennium Bridge: Take a leisurely walk hand in hand along the picturesque Millennium Bridge, which spans the Morača River. The bridge provides breathtaking views of the cityscape and surrounding mountains, resulting in a romantic atmosphere. Enjoy a truly romantic evening by watching the sunset or the city lights.

2. Explore the Old Town: Spend a romantic afternoon exploring Podgorica's Old Town (Stara Varoš). Wander through the narrow streets, admire the historic architecture, and find hidden gems together. Visit cozy cafes, charming boutiques, and local craft shops. The intimate and rustic setting of the Old Town is ideal for creating romantic moments.

3. Visit Niagara Falls: Niagara Falls, located just outside Podgorica, is a stunning natural attraction with a serene and romantic atmosphere. To get to the cascading waterfalls, take a short hike through the lush greenery. Enjoy the tranquility of the surroundings, have a picnic by the water, and capture some beautiful memories together.

4. Have a Romantic Dinner: Podgorica has a number of restaurants that offer a romantic atmosphere for a special dinner. Choose a restaurant with a cozy atmosphere, candlelit tables, and a menu that includes local or international flavors. Eat a delicious meal while enjoying each other's company and making lasting memories.

5. Take a Boat Ride on Lake Skadar: Lake Skadar, near Podgorica, provides a romantic getaway surrounded by nature. Rent a boat or take a guided tour to explore the lake's tranquil waters. Cruise along the coast, admire the breathtaking scenery, and keep an eye out for wildlife. It's a peaceful and romantic escape from the hustle and bustle of city life.

6. Visit Dajbabe Monastery: The Dajbabe Monastery is a one-of-a-kind and picturesque monastery nestled within a cave surrounded by lush greenery. Visit this peaceful and spiritual location with your partner and take a moment to appreciate the serene atmosphere. The monastery's serene surroundings and stunning architecture make it an ideal romantic getaway location.

7. Go Wine Tasting: Montenegro is well-known for its excellent wines, and Podgorica is an excellent location for a group wine tasting. Visit a local winery or wine bar and try different wines, paired with local cheeses and delicacies. Learn about the winemaking process, appreciate the flavors, and enjoy each other's company in a romantic environment.

8. Take a Horseback Ride in the Countryside: Get away from the city and go on a romantic horseback ride through the beautiful Montenegrin countryside. Several equestrian centers near Podgorica offer guided rides for riders of various skill levels. Enjoy the peace and quiet of nature, breathe in the fresh air, and appreciate the scenic landscapes while sharing this one-of-a-kind experience with your partner.

9. Picnic in Gorica Park: Gorica Park is a picturesque urban park on the outskirts of Podgorica. Find a cozy spot in the shade of the trees, spread out a blanket, and enjoy a romantic picnic with your loved one. Bring some tasty local treats, wine, or champagne to make the experience even more memorable. After that, take a leisurely stroll through the park's trails and admire its natural beauty.

10. Enjoy the Sunset from Ljubović Hill: Ljubović Hill provides a panoramic view of Podgorica, making it an ideal spot to watch the sunset with your partner. Take a quick hike up the hill, find a comfortable spot, and watch the sky transform into a canvas of vibrant colors. It's a romantic and awe-inspiring experience that you can share while taking in the beauty of nature.

These romantic activities in Podgorica allow you to create cherished memories with your partner.

Whether you're exploring the city's charming neighborhoods, admiring nature's beauty, or enjoying a romantic dinner, Podgorica has plenty of options to make your time together truly memorable.

Budget Things To Do At Podgorica.

If you're looking for budget-friendly activities in Podgorica, there are several options that allow you to explore the city and its surroundings without breaking the bank. Here are some budget things to do in Podgorica:

1. Explore the City Center: Take a walking tour of Podgorica's city center to learn about its history, culture, and architecture. Visit notable sites such as the Clock Tower, the Cathedral of the Resurrection of Christ, and Republic Square. Enjoy the city's vibrant atmosphere and visit the many free or low-cost attractions, such as public parks and gardens.

2. Visit Museums and Galleries: Podgorica has a number of museums and galleries that provide free or low-cost admission. The Museum of Contemporary Art exhibits modern and contemporary artworks, while the Natural History Museum provides information about Montenegro's diverse flora and fauna. Take advantage of this opportunity to immerse yourself in art, history, and culture while remaining within your budget.

3. Hike to Gorica Hill: For those who enjoy the outdoors, hiking to Gorica Hill is an excellent choice. The hill is easily accessible from the city center and provides a panoramic view of Podgorica. Lace up your walking shoes, pack a picnic, and head to the summit. Enjoy the fresh air, nature, and breathtaking views at no cost.

4. Relax in the Parks: Podgorica has many parks and green spaces where you can relax and enjoy nature. The Park Forest Gorica is a popular destination with walking paths, benches, and picnic areas. Park Njegoševa offers a peaceful setting with stunning views of the city. Spend a relaxing afternoon in one of these parks, reading a book or having a picnic while enjoying nature.

5. Visit Lake Skadar: Lake Skadar, near Podgorica, is the largest lake in the Balkans and boasts breathtaking natural beauty. While boat tours and guided excursions can be expensive, you can still visit the lake on a budget. Pack a picnic and visit one of the lake's public beaches, such as Virpazar or Murici, to swim, sunbathe, and enjoy the beautiful scenery.

6. Explore Podgorica's Old Town: Stara Varoš is a charming neighborhood with narrow streets and historic buildings. Explore the area at your own pace, taking in the atmosphere and admiring the architecture. Explore the historic Clock Tower and the remnants of the Ribnica Fortress. This self-guided tour of the Old Town is free and provides insight into the city's history.

7. Attend Local Events: Keep an eye out for local events and festivals taking place in Podgorica during your visit. Many of these events, such as cultural performances, music concerts, and street festivals, are free or charge a small admission fee. Check local listings or ask residents for recommendations to find these low-cost cultural experiences.

Taking advantage of these low-cost activities in Podgorica allows you to enjoy the city's attractions, nature, and culture without breaking the bank. There are numerous options for having a memorable and affordable time in Podgorica, including exploring the city center, visiting parks, and participating in local events.

Best Budget Things to Do in Podgorica.

1. Take a leisurely walk around Podgorica's city center. Explore landmarks such as Independence Square, the Clock Tower, and the Millennium Bridge. Enjoy the architecture, street art, and lively atmosphere without spending a dime.

2. Visit Museums and Galleries: Podgorica has a number of museums and galleries that provide free or low-cost admission. To learn more about Montenegrin history, art, and culture, visit the Museum of Contemporary Art, the Natural History Museum, or the King Nikola Castle Museum.

3. Visit the Park of the Revolution: Located near the city center, the Park of the Revolution is a tranquil green space with walking paths and benches. Spend some time relaxing in nature, having a picnic, or reading a book.

4. Hike to Gorica Hill: Put on your walking shoes and head up Gorica Hill, which provides panoramic views of Podgorica. Enjoy the natural beauty, take stunning photographs, and have a low-cost outdoor adventure.

5. Explore the impressive Orthodox Cathedral of the Resurrection of Christ, which is located in the city center. Admire the beautiful architecture, take in the religious art, and enjoy a moment of peace.

6. Enjoy Local Street Food: Try delicious Montenegrin street food at a reasonable price. Try "burek" (savory pastry), "ćevapi" (grilled meat), or "pljeskavica" (Balkan-style burger) from local food stalls or bakeries.

7. Relax by the Moraca River: Visit the Moraca River, which runs through Podgorica, and find a peaceful spot to unwind. Pack a blanket, bring a book, or simply relax and listen to the flowing river.

8. Attend Cultural Events: Be on the lookout for free or low-cost cultural events in Podgorica, such as concerts, art exhibitions, and festivals. These events frequently feature local talent and offer an opportunity to explore the city's cultural scene.

9. Explore the Podgorica City Stadium: If you enjoy sports, go to the Podgorica City Stadium. While there may be a fee to attend matches, you can still visit the stadium and enjoy the atmosphere when it is not in use.

10. Visit the Old Railway Bridge: Walk to the Old Railway Bridge, a historic landmark in Podgorica. Enjoy the Morača River views and take memorable photos of this architectural gem.

These inexpensive activities will allow you to enjoy the charm of Podgorica without breaking the bank. Before planning your visit, make sure to check the hours of operation and availability of attractions and events.

Best Day Trips In Podgorica.

Here are some of the best day trips you can take from Podgorica, both within the city and outside:

1. Skadar Lake: Located just a short drive from Podgorica, Skadar Lake is the largest lake in the Balkans and a natural paradise. Take a boat tour to explore the lake's stunning landscapes, spot diverse bird species, and visit charming fishing villages.

2. Ostrog Monastery: Located on a cliffside, the Ostrog Monastery is an important Orthodox pilgrimage site in Montenegro. Admire the distinctive architecture and take in the breathtaking panoramic views. It is approximately two hours from Podgorica.

3. Biogradska Gora National Park: Explore the pristine beauty of Biogradska Gora National Park. Hike through ancient forests, visit Biogradsko Lake, and enjoy the fresh mountain air. It is about a two-hour drive from Podgorica.

4. Lovćen National Park: Discover the rugged mountains, deep canyons, and breathtaking views. Climb Mount Lovćen to experience breathtaking panoramic views. It is about an hour and a half's drive from Podgorica.

5. Cetinje: Explore the historical town of Cetinje, Montenegro's former royal capital. Discover Montenegro's rich history and culture by visiting the Cetinje Monastery, the Presidential Palace, and the National Museum. Cetinje is located about 30 minutes from Podgorica.

6. Ada Bojana: If you're looking for a beach day, visit Ada Bojana, a triangular-shaped island at the mouth of the Bojana River. Relax on the sandy beaches, try water sports, and eat fresh seafood at local restaurants. It is approximately a two-hour drive from Podgorica.

7. Durmitor National Park: Take a day trip to Durmitor National Park, which is known for its spectacular mountains, glacial lakes, and hiking trails. Explore Black Lake, hike to Bobotov Kuk Peak, or simply take in the breathtaking scenery. It's about three and a half hours from Podgorica.

8. Tara River Canyon: Explore the breathtaking Tara River Canyon, which is one of the world's deepest. Enjoy white-water rafting, zip-lining, or simply admire the natural beauty of this UNESCO World Heritage Site. The drive from Podgorica takes about three hours.

9. Kotor: Visit the picturesque coastal town of Kotor, which is known for its medieval architecture and breathtaking bay views. Explore the charming narrow streets, visit the Kotor Fortress, and soak up the vibrant atmosphere. Kotor is about an hour and a half drive from Podgorica.

10. Lake Plav: Visit Lake Plav, a peaceful mountain lake surrounded by lush scenery. Take a leisurely walk along the beach, go fishing, or simply unwind in nature's tranquility. It is approximately a two-hour drive from Podgorica.

These day trips will allow you to discover Montenegro's diverse beauty, from mountains and lakes to historic towns and coastal treasures. Before embarking on day trips, make sure to plan your transportation and check the opening hours of attractions.

Best Tours to Explore Skadar Lake.

1. Undiscovered Montenegro: Undiscovered Montenegro provides various boat tours on Skadar Lake. They offer guided tours led by knowledgeable local guides who educate visitors about the lake's history, culture, and wildlife. Their tours frequently include stops at traditional fishing villages, bird-watching spots, and private swimming areas.

2. Skadar Lake Boat Trips: Skadar Lake Boat Trips is another reputable tour operator that provides boat tours of Skadar Lake. They offer guided boat tours to

showcase the lake's natural beauty and surroundings. Their tours typically include visits to monasteries, bird-watching opportunities, and traditional Montenegrin cuisine.

3. North Montenegro 4x4: North Montenegro 4x4 provides a unique combination of off-road and boat tours of Skadar Lake. Their tours include an exciting off-road drive through the surrounding mountains, followed by a relaxing boat ride on the lake. This allows you to enjoy both the picturesque scenery and the tranquil waters of Skadar Lake.

4. Montenegro Adventure: Montenegro Adventure provides boat tours that focus on discovering the wildlife and bird species of Skadar Lake. Their knowledgeable guides explain the lake's ecosystem and assist visitors in identifying and locating various bird species. These tours are perfect for nature lovers and bird watchers.

5. Skadar Lake Cruises: Skadar Lake Cruises is a local company that provides a variety of boat tours to suit different needs. They offer both group and private tours, allowing you to tailor your experience to your preferences. Their boat tours allow you to swim,

watch birds, and visit historical sites around Skadar Lake.

When booking a boat tour, consider the duration, itinerary, group size, and price to find the best option for your needs. It's also a good idea to check availability and make reservations in advance to ensure your spot on the tour.

Insider tips for the best places to stay and their proximity to attractions

1. City Center: Podgorica's city center is a popular choice for tourists due to its central location and proximity to many attractions. Staying in the city center allows you to easily visit attractions like the Millennium Bridge, Clock Tower, and Republic Square. There are also several restaurants, cafes, and shops within walking distance.

2. Stara Varoš (Old Town): This neighborhood has a charming and historic atmosphere. It is famous for its narrow streets, traditional architecture, and cultural attractions. Staying in this area gives you easy access to attractions such as Ribnica Fortress, the

Turkish Clock Tower, and the Church of the Holy Heart of Jesus.

3. Gorica Hill: For those seeking a more tranquil and scenic setting, Gorica Hill is an excellent choice. This area is located on a hill that overlooks the city and provides stunning views of Podgorica. It's a tranquil getaway with walking trails, parks, and the iconic King Nikola's Castle. It's a little further from the city center but offers a peaceful atmosphere.

4. New City: Podgorica's New City neighborhood is known for its modern architecture, shopping malls, and business districts. Staying in this area offers a more contemporary vibe with easy access to amenities such as malls, restaurants, and nightlife venues. It's a convenient location for business travelers and those who prefer a more modern setting.

5. Delta City Area: This area, which is near the Delta City shopping mall, includes both residential and commercial spaces. It's an ideal location with easy access to shopping, dining, and entertainment options. The neighborhood is well-connected to public transportation, making it simple to explore other parts of the city.

6. Zabjelo: Zabjelo is a residential neighborhood situated slightly outside of the city center. It has a quieter, more local feel, with a mix of residential buildings and small businesses. Staying in Zabjelo allows you to see how the locals live their daily lives. It is also close to Montenegro University and the Moraca Sports Center.

7. City Kvart: City Kvart is Podgorica's vibrant and upcoming neighborhood. It's known for its modern apartment buildings, trendy cafes, and vibrant nightlife. Staying in this area allows you to experience the city's modern scene and vibrant atmosphere. The National Theater and the Cathedral of the Resurrection of Christ are also within walking distance.

8. New Boulevard Area: The New Boulevard, also known as Novi Bulevar, is a recently developed neighborhood in Podgorica. It has large boulevards, modern buildings, and green spaces. Staying in this area provides a modern and spacious environment, and it is close to the City Stadium, Millennium Bridge, and Mall of Montenegro.

9. *Preko Morače*: This neighborhood is located across the Morača River from the city center. It includes a mix of residential neighborhoods, parks, and cultural institutions. Staying in this area offers a relaxed atmosphere within walking distance of attractions like the Natural History Museum and Petrović Castle.

10. *Tuzi: Tuzi is a small town situated*

When deciding where to stay in Podgorica, think about your preferences and the proximity to the attractions you want to see. Each area has its own distinct charm and advantages, so prioritize what is most important to you in terms of convenience, atmosphere, and proximity to the destinations you want to visit.

Information on amenities, facilities, and booking options

1. *Amenities:* Accommodations in Podgorica typically provide a variety of amenities to ensure a

pleasant stay. Free Wi-Fi, air conditioning, en-suite bathrooms, flat-screen televisions, and complimentary toiletries are all standard amenities. Some accommodations may also offer extra amenities such as on-site restaurants, bars, fitness centers, and parking.

2. *Facilities:* Depending on the type of accommodation you choose, you will have access to a variety of amenities to help you enjoy your stay. Hotels frequently provide services like 24-hour front desk assistance, room service, concierge services, and luggage storage. Hostels may have communal kitchens, common areas, laundromats, and lockers. Apartments and guesthouses may have self-catering facilities, such as fully equipped kitchens or kitchenettes.

3. *Booking Options:* There are several ways to book accommodations in Podgorica. You can book directly on the hotel, hostel, or lodging's official website, or by phone or email. Many accommodations offer online booking platforms where you can check availability, compare prices, and make reservations. Popular online travel agencies and booking websites,

such as Booking.com, Expedia, and Airbnb, also provide a variety of lodging options in Podgorica.

4. Payment: Most accommodations in Podgorica accept credit cards, but some may accept cash. It is a good idea to check the accepted payment methods ahead of time and have the appropriate payment option available during your stay. Before you arrive, make sure you clarify any specific payment requirements or policies with the accommodation provider.

5. Seasonal Considerations: Podgorica's peak tourist season occurs in the summer months, particularly in July and August, when the weather is warm. To secure your preferred accommodation during this period, book well in advance. Prices may also rise during peak season, so booking early can help you get a better deal.

When booking accommodations in Podgorica, keep your preferences, budget, and desired amenities in mind. Researching and comparing options ahead of time can help you find the best accommodation that meets your needs while also improving your overall experience in the city.

CHAPTER 11:

PRACTICAL INFORMATION AND TRAVEL TIPS

Essential information about local customs, etiquette, and safety precautions

Here's some essential information about local customs, etiquette, and safety precautions in Podgorica, as if you're receiving advice from a local with experience:

1. Greetings and Etiquette: When meeting someone in Podgorica, it is customary to extend a handshake and make eye contact. It is also considered polite to address people by their titles and surnames unless given permission to use their first names. Montenegrins appreciate polite and respectful behavior.

2. Public Displays of Affection: Montenegrin society is more conservative about public displays of affection. Holding hands is generally acceptable, but excessive displays of affection should be avoided in public places.

3. Dining Etiquette: When dining in Podgorica, it is customary to wait until the host or the eldest person at the table starts eating before proceeding. It's also customary to keep your hands visible on the table while eating and finish everything on your plate as a show of appreciation.

4. Dress Code: Although Podgorica has a casual dress code, it is recommended that you dress modestly when visiting religious sites or more formal establishments. Cover your shoulders and knees when entering churches or mosques, and take off your shoes if necessary.

5. Safety Precautions: Although Podgorica is generally a safe city, it is always advisable to take common-sense safety precautions. Keep an eye on your belongings in crowded areas, avoid displaying expensive items, and take reliable transportation. It is also recommended to stay in well-lit and populated areas, particularly at night.

6. Drinking Water: Tap water in Podgorica is generally safe to consume. If you prefer, you can buy bottled water, which is readily available in stores and supermarkets.

7. Transportation: Podgorica's public transportation system includes buses and taxis. Buses are an easy and inexpensive way to get around the city. When taking a taxi, make sure the driver uses a meter or agrees on a price before beginning the trip.

8. Language: The official language of Podgorica is Montenegrin. While English is widely spoken in tourist areas and among younger generations, learning a few basic Montenegrin phrases, such as greetings and simple expressions, can be useful.

9. Currency: Podgorica's official currency is the Euro (€). Most establishments accept credit cards, but it's a good idea to have some cash on hand for small purchases and in case of card payment issues.

10. Emergency Numbers: Dial 112 for general emergencies and 122 for police assistance. These numbers can be used in any emergency situation that necessitates immediate action.

Remember to always be respectful, open-minded, and aware of local customs and traditions. This will ensure that your visit to Podgorica is more enriching and enjoyable.

Transportation tips within the city

1. Public Buses: Podgorica has a dependable public bus system that serves several areas of the city. Buses provide an affordable and convenient mode of transportation. Bus stops can be found throughout the city, and route and schedule information is usually displayed at each stop. It is recommended that you bring small change or a transportation card to pay for your fare.

2. Taxis: Taxis are readily available in Podgorica and can be a convenient mode of transportation, particularly if you're traveling with luggage or in a hurry. Look for licensed taxis with a visible taxi sign on the roof and a prominently displayed identification number. It's a good idea to ask the driver to use the meter or agree on a price before beginning your journey.

3. Walking: Podgorica is a small city, so many of the main attractions, shops, and restaurants are within walking distance of one another, particularly in the city center. Walking allows you to explore the city at your own pace and discover hidden gems along the way.

4. Cycling: Cycling is gaining popularity in Podgorica, and the city is working to improve its cycling infrastructure. Bicycles can be rented from a variety of rental shops or used in the city's bike-sharing program, if available. Cycling is an excellent way to explore the city, especially in areas with designated bike lanes and paths.

5. Ride-Sharing Apps: Uber and Bolt are available in Podgorica. These apps enable you to book a ride with a private driver using your smartphone. They frequently provide convenient and dependable transportation, and the app allows you to track the driver's location and make cashless payments.

6. Car Rental: If you prefer the freedom of having your own car, car rental services are available in Podgorica. Renting a car allows you to explore the city and its surroundings at your own pace. However, keep in mind that traffic in the city center can be congested, and parking may be limited in certain areas.

7. Traffic and Parking: Podgorica has traffic congestion, especially during peak hours. Plan your trips accordingly, taking traffic into consideration. If you're driving, be aware of parking rules and available parking spaces. Some locations may have parking meters, while others may require a parking permit. It is best to park in designated parking lots or garages to avoid fines and towing.

8. Navigation: Having a map or a navigation app on your smartphone can help you get around Podgorica. Most major streets are well-marked, with road signs in both Cyrillic and Latin alphabets.

Using these transportation tips, you'll be able to easily navigate Podgorica and make the most of your time exploring the city.

Emergency contacts and medical facilities

Here is some information about emergency contacts and medical facilities in Podgorica:

Emergency Contacts:

1. General Emergency: In case of any emergency requiring immediate assistance, dial 112. This number can be used to reach police, fire department, or medical services.

2. Police: If you need to report a crime or require police assistance, you can dial 122 to reach the local police station in Podgorica.

3. Ambulance and Medical Emergency: For medical emergencies and ambulance services, dial 124. This number will connect you to the emergency medical services in Podgorica.

4. Podgorica Clinical Center: The Clinical Center of Montenegro, located in Podgorica, is a major medical institution that provides specialized medical care and emergency services. Contact information for the Clinical Center of Montenegro:

- Address: Ljubljanska bb, 81000 Podgorica
- Phone: +382 20 412 000
- Website: http://www.kccg.me/

5. *Poison Control Center:* If there is a case of poisoning or you require immediate advice regarding poisoning, you can contact the Poison Control Center at +382 20 242 333.

Medical Facilities:

1. *Podgorica Clinical Center:* The Clinical Center of Montenegro in Podgorica is a leading medical institution in the city, providing various medical specializations, emergency services, and advanced medical treatments.

2. *Private Clinics:* Podgorica has several private clinics and medical centers that offer a range of medical services. Some well-known private clinics in Podgorica include:
  - Medigroup Clinic Podgorica
  - Euromedik Podgorica
  - CM Medicus Podgorica

3. *Pharmacies:* Pharmacies, known as "apoteka" in Montenegrin, can be found throughout Podgorica.

171

They offer over-the-counter medications, prescription drugs, and basic healthcare supplies. Some pharmacies may be open 24 hours a day for emergencies. Look for the green cross sign to find a pharmacy.

When visiting a foreign country, it is always advisable to have travel insurance that covers medical emergencies. If you require medical assistance, call the local emergency services or go to the nearest medical facility for prompt care.

Useful phrases and basic Montenegrin language guide

Here are some useful phrases and a basic Montenegrin language guide to help you communicate in Podgorica:

1. Greetings:
   Hello: Zdravo (ZDRAH-voh)
   Good morning: Dobro jutro (DOH-bro YOO-troh)
   Good afternoon: Dobar dan (DOH-bahr dahn)
   Good evening: Dobro veče (DOH-bro VEH-cheh)
   Goodbye: Doviđenja (doh-VEE-jeh-nyah)
   Thank you: Hvala (HVAH-lah)

You're welcome: Nema na čemu (NEH-mah nah CHEH-moo)

2. Basic Expressions:

Yes: Da (dah)

No: Ne (neh)

Please: Molim (MOH-leem)

Excuse me: Izvinite (eez-VEE-nee-teh)

I'm sorry: Žao mi je (zhah-oh mee yeh)

Do you speak English?: Govorite li engleski? (GOH-voh-ree-teh lee ENG-les-kee?)

- I don't understand: Ne razumijem (neh rah-ZOO-mee-yem)

3. Numbers:

- One: Jedan (YEH-dahn)
- Two: Dva (dvah)
- Three: Tri (tree)
- Four: Četiri (CHEH-tee-ree)
- Five: Pet (peht)
- Ten: Deset (DEH-set)

4. Directions:

- Where is...?: Gdje je...? (gd-yeh yeh)
- Left: Lijevo (lee-YEH-voh)
- Right: Desno (DEHS-noh)

- Straight ahead: Pravo (PRAH-voh)
- Bus station: Autobuska stanica (ow-TOH-boos-kah STAH-nee-tsah)
- Train station: Željeznička stanica (ZHEH-lyehz-neech-kah STAH-nee-tsah)
- Airport: Aerodrom (ah-EH-roh-drom)

5. Ordering Food and Drinks:

- I would like...: Ja bih želio/željela... (yah bee ZHEH-lyoh/ZHEH-lyeh-lah)
- A table for two, please: Sto za dvoje, molim (stoh zah DVOH-yeh, MOH-leem)
- Water: Voda (VOH-dah)
- Beer: Pivo (PEE-voh)
- Wine: Vino (VEE-noh)
- Menu: Meni (MEH-nee)

Remember that most people in Podgorica, particularly in tourist areas, speak English. However, attempting to speak a few basic phrases in Montenegrin can impress the locals and improve your overall experience.

Please let me know if you would like to make any specific additions, modifications, or if you have any preferences for the subsequent chapters.

CHAPTER 12.

PERFECT 7 DAY ITINERARY FOR FIRST TIME TRAVELERS TO PODGORICA.

Day 1: Arrival and City Exploration

Morning.

Upon arrival at Podgorica Airport, proceed to the city center and check into your accommodation. Allow some time to freshen up and settle in.

Begin your exploration of Podgorica by visiting Stara Varoš, the city's historic Old Town. As you walk through its narrow cobblestone streets, you'll feel transported back in time. Admire the well-preserved Ottoman-era architecture, which features stone buildings with red-tiled roofs and intricate wooden balconies. The atmosphere is enchanting, with bright colors and charming details around every corner.

Take a leisurely stroll through the Old Town, making sure to see the iconic Clock Tower, which is a symbol of Podgorica's history. Climb to the top of the tower for a panoramic view of the surroundings. From this vantage point, you can appreciate the contrast between the historic buildings and the modern cityscape that has developed around them.

Sahat Kula Fortress, located a short walk from the Clock Tower, awaits your exploration. This fortress from the 16th century provides a glimpse into Podgorica's defensive past. Explore its grounds and imagine the stories of battles and conquests that occurred within its walls.

After immersing yourself in history, head to the city center and visit Independence Square (Trg Nezavisnosti). This bustling square is a hub of activity and an excellent place to soak up the local culture. Observe how locals go about their daily lives, and perhaps find a cozy café to enjoy a cup of Montenegrin coffee or a refreshing drink.

Afternoon: Have lunch at one of the city center's many restaurants, which offer a variety of cuisine. Montenegrin cuisine combines Mediterranean and Balkan flavors, so try local specialties like Ćevapi (grilled minced meat), Njeguški pršut (smoked ham), and Kacamak (a hearty cornmeal dish).

Following lunch, continue your city exploration by crossing the iconic Millennium Bridge. This modern architectural marvel spans the Morača River, offering breathtaking views of the surrounding area. Take a leisurely stroll along the bridge, and don't forget to take photos of the picturesque riverbanks and city skyline.

From the Millennium Bridge, proceed to Gorica Park, a tranquil green oasis on the opposite bank of the river. This park provides a refreshing escape from the urban bustle as well as stunning views of the city. Take a leisurely stroll along the pathways, relax on one of the benches, or simply enjoy the peacefulness of nature.

Evening: As the sun sets, return to the city center to explore the vibrant streets filled with shops, cafes, and restaurants. Take your time exploring local boutiques and souvenir shops, where you can find one-of-a-kind items like traditional handicrafts, locally produced wines, and handcrafted jewelry.

For dinner, indulge in Podgorica's vibrant culinary scene. The city has a wide variety of dining options, from traditional Montenegrin cuisine to international flavors. Choose a restaurant that piques your interest and enjoy a delicious meal paired with a glass of local wine or a refreshing Montenegrin beer.

After dinner, take a relaxing evening stroll along the Morača River promenade. The illuminated bridges and buildings create a magical atmosphere, ideal for a romantic stroll or a quiet moment of reflection.

As your first day in Podgorica comes to an end, take advantage of the opportunity to relax and unwind in the comfort of your accommodations. Reflect on the day's sights and experiences, and prepare for the adventures that lie ahead.

Remember to check the opening hours of attractions and restaurants, as they may change. Additionally, customize this itinerary based on your personal preferences and any specific events or festivals taking place during your visit to Podgorica.

Day 2: Skadar Lake and Rijeka Crnojevića

Morning:

After a hearty breakfast at your hotel, prepare for a day trip to the stunning Skadar Lake, one of Europe's largest freshwater lakes and a true natural wonder.

Make your way to Skadar Lake, which is a short distance from Podgorica. Upon arrival, take a boat tour to enjoy the lake's stunning landscapes, abundant wildlife, and charming villages.

As you cruise along the tranquil waters, prepare to be captivated by the natural beauty that surrounds you. Skadar Lake is known for its pristine nature, which includes lush greenery, rugged cliffs, and crystal-clear waters. Skadar Lake is a designated bird sanctuary, so keep an eye out for a variety of bird species, such as pelicans, herons, and cormorants.

Take in the tranquility of the surroundings and the fresh air as your boat glides through the lake's hidden corners. Your knowledgeable guide will provide fascinating insights into the lake's ecology, history, and cultural significance.

After the boat tour, visit the picturesque village of Rijeka Crnojevića, situated on the Crnojević River. This charming village provides a peaceful setting and insight into Montenegro's rural lifestyle.

Take a leisurely stroll along the riverbanks, soaking up the peaceful atmosphere and admiring the traditional stone houses that line the shore. Cross the old stone bridge, which provides stunning views of the river and surrounding landscape.

For lunch, find a cozy local restaurant and eat traditional Montenegrin cuisine. Try fresh lake fish paired with local wines or refreshing beverages. The region's culinary specialties are distinguished by their simplicity and use of high-quality, locally sourced ingredients.

After lunch, consider a quick hike to the nearby Pavlova Strana viewpoint. This vantage point provides breathtaking panoramic views of the river winding through the valley, framed by rugged mountains in the background. It's an ideal location for taking memorable photographs while also immersing yourself in the region's natural beauty.

In the evening, return to Podgorica and enjoy the scenic views along the way. When you arrive in the city, you can spend the evening exploring its vibrant nightlife and dining options.

Podgorica has a variety of dining options, ranging from cozy local restaurants serving traditional Montenegrin cuisine to trendy international eateries. Take your time selecting a restaurant that suits your tastes and enjoy a delicious dinner while savoring the flavors and culinary traditions of the region.

After dinner, you can relax and unwind at a local bar, sipping on a refreshing drink or taking in the city's lively atmosphere. Alternatively, take a leisurely evening stroll through the city center, exploring the illuminated streets and absorbing the vibrant atmosphere.

As the day comes to an end, return to your lodging and take some time to rest and recharge for the adventures that await you the next day.

Prior to your visit, check the availability and timing of Skadar Lake boat tours, as they may vary depending on the season and weather conditions. Pack sunscreen, comfortable walking shoes, and a camera to capture the beauty of Skadar Lake and Rijeka Crnojevića.

Day 3: Ostrog Monastery and Cetinje

Morning:
After breakfast, prepare for a day of cultural and spiritual exploration, including visits to the famous Ostrog Monastery and the historical town of Cetinje.

Begin your journey by traveling from Podgorica to the Ostrog Monastery, which is nestled high in the mountains. The monastery is an important pilgrimage site and a work of religious architecture. As you ascend the winding road, prepare to be astounded by the breathtaking views of the surrounding scenery.

When you arrive at the monastery, take a moment to admire the breathtaking scenery. The Ostrog Monastery is built into the vertical cliffs of Ostroška Greda, creating a breathtaking sight. The monastery complex is divided into two sections: Upper Monastery and Lower Monastery.

Take a guided tour of the monastery, discovering its intricate frescoes, religious artifacts, and sacred spaces. The Upper Monastery houses the tomb of St. Basil of Ostrog, the monastery's patron and a revered saint. The Lower Monastery houses a church dedicated to the Holy Cross and provides a peaceful setting for prayer and reflection.

Your knowledgeable guide will explain the fascinating history and legends surrounding Ostrog Monastery. The monastery draws visitors from all religious backgrounds, and its spiritual significance is palpable.

After visiting the Ostrog Monastery, travel to the historic town of Cetinje, Montenegro's former royal capital. Cetinje is renowned for its rich cultural heritage and architectural treasures.

Upon arrival in Cetinje, take a walking tour of the town's highlights. Begin at the Cetinje Monastery, a grand Orthodox Christian monastery dating back to the fifteenth century. Explore the ornate interior, which features stunning frescoes and religious icons.

Next, go to the Cetinje National Museum, which is housed in the former royal palace. The museum displays Montenegro's history and culture through a vast collection of artifacts such as artwork, weaponry, and royal regalia. Learn about Montenegro's history and the significant role Cetinje played in its development.

Explore the town's main boulevard, Njegoševa Street, which features historic buildings, cafes, and shops. Admire the elegant architecture and visit King Nikola's Palace, a stunning residence that once housed the Montenegrin royal family.

Evening: Return to Podgorica and relax. You may decide to take advantage of the city's cultural offerings, such as visiting art galleries or attending a theatre performance.

Alternatively, spend a relaxing evening at one of Podgorica's local spas or wellness centres. After a day of exploring, pamper yourself with a rejuvenating massage or relax in a sauna to allow your body and mind to recharge.

For dinner, visit one of Podgorica's many culinary establishments, where you can savor delicious Montenegrin cuisine or sample international flavors. Enjoy traditional dishes like Njeguški cheese, prosciutto, and meat stews, paired with regional wines or refreshing beverages.

After dinner, take a leisurely stroll along the Morača River promenade to enjoy the illuminated cityscape and reflect on the day. Alternatively, find a cozy café or bar to unwind, socialize, and take in the vibrant atmosphere of Podgorica's nightlife.

As the day comes to a close, return to your lodging and prepare for the next day's adventures while reflecting on the cultural and spiritual encounters you had at Ostrog Monastery and Cetinje.

When visiting religious sites, it is best to dress modestly and respectfully. Also, check the opening hours of the Ostrog Monastery and the Cetinje National Museum, as they may differ. Bring comfortable walking shoes, as there will be a lot of walking throughout the day.

Day 4: Durmitor National Park and Tara River Canyon

Morning:
After breakfast, prepare for an exciting day of outdoor exploration as you visit Durmitor National Park and the stunning Tara River Canyon.

Depart from Podgorica and travel to Durmitor National Park, a UNESCO World Heritage site known for its breathtaking scenery and outdoor recreational opportunities. As you approach the park, you'll be met with the towering peaks of the Durmitor mountain range and the pristine beauty of the surrounding wilderness.

Begin your adventure by visiting the Black Lake (Crno Jezero), one of Durmitor's most famous landmarks. Take a leisurely hike around the lake, surrounded by dense forests and beautiful mountain scenery. Inhale the fresh mountain air and enjoy the peaceful surroundings.

Explore Durmitor National Park further by visiting nearby Žabljak, the Balkans' highest town. This charming alpine town is an ideal base for outdoor enthusiasts, offering a variety of activities such as hiking, mountain biking, and skiing.

Explore Žabljak's quaint streets and enjoy the mountainous atmosphere. You'll find cozy restaurants and cafes where you can grab a bite to eat

or sip coffee while admiring th
mountains.

Afternoon: Explore the breathtaking 'ι
Canyon, also known as the "Grand Ca
Europe." This natural wonder is Europe's ι
canyon, with breathtaking views that will leave
in awe.

Take a scenic drive along the canyon's winding roads,
which offer breathtaking views at every turn. Admire
the sheer vertical cliffs that drop into the crystal-clear
turquoise waters of the Tara River below. Keep your
camera handy so you can capture the canyon's
breathtaking views and rugged natural beauty.

Consider going on a thrilling rafting trip down the
Tara River for an adrenaline rush. The river's rapids
and cascading waterfalls provide an exhilarating
experience as you navigate through the canyon's
dramatic scenery. Rafting trips are available for a
variety of skill levels, ensuring a memorable
adventure for everyone.

If you prefer a more relaxed experience, you can
simply admire the scenery from designated

viewpoints along the canyon's rim. Take your time admiring the natural beauty and appreciating the untouched wilderness that surrounds you.

Evening: Return to Podgorica and reflect on the day's outdoor activities. When you return to the city, take the evening to relax and reflect on the incredible natural wonders you've seen.

For dinner, discover Podgorica's culinary scene and select from a variety of restaurants serving both local and international cuisine. Try dishes inspired by Montenegrin traditions, such as hearty stews, grilled meats, or fresh seafood, paired with regional wines or craft beers.

After dinner, enjoy a stroll through one of Podgorica's parks, such as Park Njegoševa or Park Zelena Gora. These green spaces provide a peaceful environment ideal for relaxation and reflection.

If you're looking for cultural experiences, check out the city's event listings for concerts, performances, and art exhibitions. Podgorica has a vibrant arts and cultural scene, and you might come across an event that interests you.

As you retire for the night, reflect on the day's adventures and plan your final day in Montenegro.

Plan your visit to Durmitor National Park and the Tara River Canyon around the activities and attractions that interest you the most. Check the weather and bring appropriate clothing and footwear for outdoor activities. If you go rafting, make sure you have the proper equipment and follow all safety instructions provided by experienced guides.

Day 5: Bay of Kotor and Perast

Morning:
On your final day in Montenegro, visit the breathtaking Bay of Kotor, known as Europe's southernmost fjord. This UNESCO World Heritage site is known for its breathtaking natural beauty, quaint coastal towns, and rich cultural heritage.

Begin your day by traveling from Podgorica to the town of Kotor, located at the bay's southernmost point. Once you arrive, take a leisurely stroll through the town's narrow, winding streets, which are lined with ancient stone buildings and picturesque squares.

Make your way to the fortified Old Town, which is surrounded by medieval walls and guarded by the imposing Kotor Fortress. Climb up the fortress walls to enjoy panoramic views of the bay and surrounding mountains. The hike to the top is strenuous but rewarding, providing an opportunity to immerse yourself in history while enjoying breathtaking views.

After leaving the fortress, explore the maze-like streets of the Old Town. Discover hidden alleys, charming squares, and historic landmarks such as St. Tryphon's Cathedral, a magnificent Romanesque church from the 12th century.

Afternoon: Explore the Bay of Kotor with a visit to Perast, an idyllic town. This small town is known for its well-preserved Venetian architecture and picturesque setting, nestled between mountains and a bay.

When you arrive in Perast, take a leisurely walk along the waterfront promenade, admiring the breathtaking views of the bay and the two picturesque islets, Our Lady of the Rocks and St. George. Consider taking a boat tour to see the islets and learn about their fascinating history and legends.

Explore the town's narrow streets, which are lined with elegant palaces and quaint stone houses. Visit the Maritime Museum to learn about Perast's maritime heritage and role as a prominent seafaring town.

For lunch, find a cozy restaurant or café that serves fresh seafood and local specialties. Enjoy dishes like black risotto, grilled fish, or octopus salad with a glass of local wine or a refreshing beverage.

In the evening, return to Podgorica and enjoy the scenic views along the way. When you arrive in the city, you can enjoy the evening at your leisure.

Consider visiting one of Podgorica's cultural institutions, such as the Montenegrin National Theatre or the Montenegrin Art Gallery, to become acquainted with the local arts scene. Attend a performance or browse the exhibitions featuring the works of Montenegrin artists and performers.

Alternatively, you may want to return to some of your favorite Podgorica spots, such as a cozy café or a local bar, to unwind and soak up the city's vibrant atmosphere. Reflect on the memories you made while traveling through Montenegro, savoring the flavors, sights, and experiences you encountered.

As the day comes to a close, return to your accommodation and spend some time packing and preparing for your departure the next day, remembering your unforgettable adventures in Montenegro.

Note: Plan your trip to the Bay of Kotor and Perast based on your interests and preferences. Consider bringing comfortable walking shoes, sunscreen, and a camera to capture the bay's beauty and surroundings. Check the opening hours of attractions and boat schedules to the islets, as these may change depending on the season.

Day 6: Departure from Montenegro

Morning:

On your final day in Montenegro, make the most of your morning before leaving by exploring more of Podgorica or participating in last-minute activities.

If you have any extra time in Podgorica, consider visiting one of the city's famous landmarks, such as the Millennium Bridge or the Clock Tower. Explore local shops and boutiques or relax in one of the city's parks, like Park Njegoševa or Park Zelena Gora.

Alternatively, if you want to spend one last time in nature, consider visiting Lake Skadar, the Balkans' largest lake. Take a boat tour around the lake, explore the diverse flora and fauna, and relax in this beautiful natural setting. Keep an eye out for different bird species, such as pelicans and herons.

As the afternoon approaches, it's time to say goodbye to Montenegro. Depending on your itinerary, arrange for transportation to the airport or your next destination. If you have some extra time before your departure, you can have a leisurely lunch at a local restaurant, savoring the flavors of Montenegrin cuisine for the last time.

Before you leave, take a moment to reflect on your journey and the unforgettable experiences you had in Montenegro. Remember the breathtaking scenery, the rich history and culture, and the warm hospitality of the Montenegrins.

If you have any leftover Montenegrin currency, exchange it for your home currency or keep it as a souvenir. Make sure you have all of your travel documents, including your passport and any necessary visas, readily available.

As you leave Montenegro, reflect on the memories and experiences you've had there. Whether you're returning home or continuing your travels, take a moment to appreciate Montenegro's natural beauty and diversity, as well as its people's warmth.

If you have a long flight or journey ahead of you, pack some snacks and entertainment to keep you comfortable. Take this opportunity to reflect on your adventures, look through your photos, and plan future trips to see more of the world.

As you leave Montenegro, carry the spirit of adventure and cultural discovery with you, knowing that you have witnessed the wonders of this enchanting country.

Plan your morning activities around your departure time, and consider any travel logistics for your next destination. It's always a good idea to check the most recent information on transportation options and flight schedules.

Day 7: Optional Extension or Departure

Morning:

On day 7, you have the option of staying in Montenegro and exploring its wonders or preparing to leave. Here are some ideas for how to spend your final day in Montenegro:

1. Coastal Exploration: If you haven't yet had the opportunity to explore Montenegro's breathtaking coastline, consider visiting popular coastal towns like Budva or Herceg Novi. Relax on the beautiful sandy beaches, swim in the crystal-clear waters of the Adriatic Sea, and soak up the lively atmosphere of these vibrant coastal destinations.

2. Lovćen National Park: A must-see for nature lovers and hikers. The park is home to Mount Lovćen, which offers breathtaking panoramic views of the surrounding mountains and the Bay of Kotor. Hike to Jezerski Vrh, the park's highest peak, and visit the mausoleum of Petar II Petrović-Njegoš, a famous Montenegrin poet and ruler.

3. Skadar Lake National Park: If you enjoy nature, pay a visit to Skadar Lake National Park, which is known for its diverse wildlife and beautiful scenery. Take a boat tour on the lake to see different bird species, explore charming lakeside villages, and relax in this beautiful natural setting.

Afternoon: Depending on your morning activity, spend the afternoon exploring or returning to Podgorica to prepare for departure.

If you're staying longer, take the time to fully immerse yourself in your chosen activity or destination, whether it's relaxing on the beach, hiking through the mountains, or admiring Skadar Lake's natural beauty.

If you're leaving Montenegro, use the afternoon to pack your belongings, pay any outstanding bills, and check out of your accommodation. Double-check your travel documents, such as your passport, tickets, and any necessary visas, to ensure a smooth departure.

Spend your final evening in Montenegro with a delicious dinner at a local restaurant. Enjoy the flavors of Montenegrin cuisine, including grilled seafood, hearty stews, and locally sourced cheese and prosciutto.

If you have some free time, take a leisurely stroll through the streets of Podgorica or find a cozy bar to relax and reflect on your time in Montenegro. Immerse yourself in the local culture, interact with the locals, or simply spend the evening reflecting on the memories you've created.

Plan your day 7 activities around your personal preferences, travel plans, and available time. Consider any necessary logistics, such as transportation, attraction hours, and distance from your accommodations. If you have a flight or another destination to visit, always give yourself enough time to get there.

Printed in Great Britain
by Amazon